Mary Haskell F

HASTINGS IN PEACE AND WAR
1930 - 1945

ISBN 1-870096-06-1

𝓕𝓟

FERNDALE PRESS

I dedicate this book to my parents, Eddie and Poll.

First published in 2002 by Ferndale Press
Copyright © 2002 Mary Porter

By the same author:
Heroes, Villains and Others from Hastings, Ferndale Press 1999
More Heroes, Villains and Others from Hastings, Ferndale Press 2000

All rights reserved. No part of this book may be reproduced, stored in a retrieval system, or transmitted in any form, or by any means, without written permission from Ferndale Press.

A catalogue record for this book is available from the British Library.

Printed by Chandlers Printers Ltd,
Saxon Mews, Reginald Road,
Bexhill-on-Sea, East Sussex TN39 3PJ

CONTENTS

page

Foreword		
Introduction		1
1	Surroundings	2
2	Law and Order	4
3	Domestic Life	7
4	Education	11
5	Transport and Travel	16
6	Leisure and Pleasure	20
7	Gathering Clouds	25
8	Sunday, 3rd September 1939	30
9	The Phoney War	32
10	The Fight Begins	37
11	Evacuation	42
12	The Bombing Starts	48
13	Shadow of Invasion	58
14	Hit and Run	66
15	The Toll Mounts	73
16	Before and after D-Day	79
17	Sunshine	87
Appendix I		91
Appendix II		92
Appendix III		93
Appendix IV		94
Appendix V		95
Appendix VI		96
Acknowledgements		97
Bibliography		98
The Author		99

FOREWORD

by
Lt. Cdr. John F. Kennett, M.B.E., R.N.(Retd.)

To those of us who lived in Hastings throughout the years of the Second World War, the clarity of this remarkable account vividly recalls the atmosphere – sounds, sights, people, events and places – that co-existed with the devastating effects of war. Amid the randomness of catastrophe, there was stoicism and the stubborn persistence of everyday life in the town.

The author sets the scene by evoking life in the thirties, prior to the onset of war. Hastings and its surroundings, its domestic life and social history, are richly described. This is local history at its best: the reader embarks on a fascinating journey that re-creates the essence of an era.

Using material drawn from documents, newspapers, personal accounts and photographs, Mary Porter has provided a local perspective on a period that shaped the lives of the British people. The meticulous research contributing to this book will prove invaluable to future historians.

This is the story of an English seaside town, but the theme of the resilience of its people, and of the human spirit, is universal.

INTRODUCTION

The past is a foreign country: they do things differently there.
(P L Hartley)

The nineteen thirties, and the wartime years that followed, were milestones which marked a childhood journey. It started in the bright days of peace, passed through deep shadow, and ended with a promise of better things to come. The corner of England where it took place was by no means exceptional, but the purpose of the book is to encapsulate the way life was lived in those times, before memories fade. The young people of today will catch a glimpse of the lives of children of a previous generation. For 'the grown-ups' who trod that same path, the conditions and events described will, perhaps, evoke many memories, and provide an opportunity to reflect on old times.

Changes, of many kinds, have taken place in Hastings since the early thirties, notably in education and policing. The war years, which accelerated many of those changes, also brought out the best and sometimes, regrettably, the worst in people. It is hoped the book will remain as a record of happenings during that period in the country's history. The conditions and events described will, doubtless, mirror those experienced by many other ordinary people in all parts of Britain. It is written from the viewpoint of someone who grew up in the County Borough of Hastings and St Leonards-on-Sea, and saw at first hand how the town was run and how, when it came up against the difficulties of war, it dealt with the practical problems and finally pulled through.

The researches for the book have revealed the work of all those local people who looked after the needs of the population, particularly in the very difficult days of the war. They were mainly council officials and police officers of great integrity and dedication to their work, who did more than they were required to do to ensure that the people of Hastings were so well served. It would perhaps not be appropriate to single out any particular group, save to say that the rescue parties who dealt with the results of the raids had, without doubt, the worst job of all. Often in imminent danger of the collapse of a building, they worked tirelessly, frequently with their bare hands, and for as long as necessary to extricate the dead and injured from the debris. The work they did must have been harrowing, to say the least, and yet they never hesitated to 'roll up their sleeves' and get on with it. The townspeople were, indeed, fortunate to have them.

Throughout the book, where a reference is made to the town of Hastings, this includes its sister area of St Leonards-on-Sea.

MHP

1
SURROUNDINGS

'Popular with visitors since 1066' as the local Information Centre likes to say, Hastings is well known for its famous battle. South-facing and sheltered from the north by the ridge of the eastern end of the South downs, it enjoys a natural climatic advantage. Following George IV's liking for the invigorating properties of sea air and bathing at Brighton, Hastings too became known as a health-giving resort which welcomed the well-to-do and even members of the Royal Family.

It became well-established as a popular seaside town and was a very pleasant place in which to live. Alfred Dyer, the Editor of the Hastings and St Leonards Observer, once wrote, *'A man must be very hard to please if he can stand on the East Hill and not be enthralled by the view of the Old Town nestling in the valley below, the modern town stretching away to the west, and the glorious cliffs and coastal scenery to the east'*.

View over the Old Town Valley from the East Hill.

In the nineteen-thirties, for most of the population of some 65,000, life was settled and went along on a fairly even keel. Incomes, though generally low, were earned in a variety of ways. Hastings had been a fishing port for centuries, and the local fishermen continued to earn their living from the sea. Their income depended on the vagaries of the weather, and their lives swung between 'feast and famine'.

Other people found employment in seasonal work revolving around the summer visitors. In 1936 for example, the town boasted a total of 16 spacious, good class hotels, 10 private hotels, innumerable guest houses, and many restaurants and cafés. A good summer season brought a lot of work and good money for those working in such places. The winters went by at a slower pace when those businesses went into semi-hibernation, and many workers became unemployed.

In the absence of manufacturing companies, regular employment for women was mostly to be found in domestic service, shops, laundries and offices. Men found stable employment with local stores or with services such as the Bus and Tram companies, the Police Force, Fire Station, Post Office, Railway Company, Gas Company, Water Works, Power Station and the Local Council. There were numerous small local shops in all areas of the town. These provided the owners and their families, who mostly lived 'over the shop', with a home and steady income. The better-qualified men and women worked in medicine, teaching, the law, local government and the civil service. It was a time when mothers rarely worked outside the home unless they were widowed, or otherwise obliged to work. In some occupations, such as teaching and the established civil service, it was usual for women to resign on marriage.

As a Borough, Hastings had its own Council, Police Force, Police Court and Education Authority. There were very good primary and secondary schools. The latter included the Boys' Grammar School and the Girls' High School, 2 good Central Schools, and Technical Schools where emphasis was on practical and manual skills. It was very much a self-contained town in charge of its own law-and-order, and day-to-day management. There was a sense of cohesion which gave the townspeople a feeling of belonging. It was 'their' town. This view of their place in things was to stand them in good stead in the years ahead.

2
LAW AND ORDER

Hastings Police Force was first set up as a paid force in 1836. When the nineteen-thirties began, the Chief Constable was Frederick James O.B.E. – a strict disciplinarian. There were many rules concerning the conduct of his men. Indeed it is clear that there was a ban on kissing whilst on duty. One unfortunate transgressor was severely reprimanded for 'kissing a married woman at West Hill, St Leonards, at 10.50 a.m. on 29.9.31, while on No. 5 beat'. (To whom the lady in question was married is not known). Prospective wives of the men were quietly vetted and expected to live exemplary lives as, incidentally, were their children. To join the police, men had to produce good character references, pass a written examination, be of sound health with good teeth, have good sight without the aid of glasses, and be of a minimum height. All were encouraged to take First Aid training, and the keen swimmers among them learnt life-saving skills which were not infrequently called upon when holiday-makers got into difficulties off the beaches.

Police Constable wearing straw summer helmet known as a 'Donkey's Breakfast'.

In the thirties, the sizeable Force consisted of The Chief Constable, a Superintendent, a number of Inspectors and Sub-Inspectors, Sergeants and Constables. Several of them were mounted police who patrolled the outlying areas around The Ridge and The East Hill. There was also a small plain-clothes (CID) section and a number of Special Constables. In 1935, the appointment of a Policewoman was approved at a wage of £2.16s (£2.80p), but up to that time the only woman employed was the Police Matron who looked after female prisoners and children in trouble. The Force was the proud possessor of two B.S.A. motorcycle combinations used for traffic patrol and dispatches. In the late thirties two eight-horsepower Morris Coupés were added.

The police did a very good job of protecting the local population and keeping them in order. The law was diligently enforced and transgressors brought before the Court without delay. Uniformed men had one complete day off a week and were employed on foot patrol to give 24-hour coverage of the whole town. They were organised into three eight-hour rotating shifts, each lasting two weeks. The shifts were worked either from 6 a.m. to 2 p.m., 2 p.m. to 10 p.m., or 10 p.m. to 6 a.m. Working in a relatively small town, the men were expected to know its geography

Clive Vale area Police Station.

intimately, and indeed they did. They also knew the habitual offenders and were quickly able to 'make enquiries' in pursuit of suspects.

The public had great confidence in, and respect for, their constabulary who dealt with all manner of offences and offenders, including beggars and vagrants. As well as the usual work of enforcing the law, they looked after lost dogs, lost children and lost property, and kept a register of all items handed in. Regular checks were made to see whether dog-owners had a licence for their animal. They were also responsible for keeping a register of all aliens living in the town.

Urgent calls to the police and other emergency services were made by pressing the emergency button in a public telephone box. There were also special free telephones set in the doors of area police stations situated around the town. These were linked directly to the main station at the rear of the Town Hall in Queens Road. From private telephones (before direct dialling) all calls of any sort were made through the operator. In an emergency, one simply asked for, 'The police please'.

Back of Town Hall showing coat of arms over the door to the Old Police Station.

The single courtroom, also in the Town Hall, adjoined the police station and was regularly used, but by today's standards far fewer serious offenders appeared there. Being brought before the court, even for a minor offence was widely regarded as a disgrace, and a prison sentence as a matter for shame.

One typical example in pre-war days concerned an inmate of the local workhouse. The man in question was charged with 'unlawfully introducing ale into the premises'. The workhouse Master gave evidence that he had, *'detected an odour emanating from the patient, which led him to suspect that the man was doing himself well'*. He ordered a watch to be kept, and the man was seen to go down a path leading to allotments at the back of the workhouse. He whistled and another man appeared who handed over a bottle. At the Police Court proceedings, the confederate confessed to the illicit act, whereupon the inmate said, *'Whatever you do, do not punish that man. Punish me. I got the beer, and I paid for it with a copper or two I had saved up'*. The inmate was fined ten shillings (50p) and given a week to pay.

By and large the townspeople were a law-abiding lot. This was largely due to the fact that, with the vigilance of the police, they knew they were unlikely 'to get away with it'. Most offences seemed to hinge around drunkenness, theft, riding a bicycle without lights, keeping a dog without a licence and strange transgressions seemingly committed in ignorance. These included making sand drawings for money on parts of the beach not designated for such activity, exhibiting performing mice within 250 yards of the sea front without a licence, and shaking mats after 9.30 a.m. Householders seldom locked their doors or windows in the day-time, or if they did, the key was left hanging inside the letter-box for the rest of the family to use. Children could play and roam freely all over the East and West Hills, in St Helen's Woods and elsewhere without adult supervision. Any odd local characters were known to children and adults alike, and either avoided or ignored.

With the approach of World War 2, the role of the police was to become greatly extended. As early as June 1936, they were given a special training course on anti-gas precautions, followed by one on air-raid precautions. Although the first of these was, thankfully, not needed, the latter most certainly was. By 1939, the County Borough of Hastings Police Force numbered 113 men and 1 woman, including a War Duties Department with responsibility for co-ordinating the A.R.P. It also had the task of charting all bombs dropped on the town including those which failed to explode.

After the outbreak of War in September 1939, as serving police officers were recalled or conscripted into the armed forces, so they were replaced with men of the War reserve. These were retired officers who were recalled to supplement the remaining men. So began the difficult years which were to lie ahead.

3
DOMESTIC LIFE

Most families in Hastings in the thirties lived in rented accommodation, and there was seldom a shortage of places to choose from. Self-contained flats and small houses were available at reasonable rents. Many of those properties still exist today, particularly in the areas adjacent to the railway line from Hastings to Ore Station. They were originally built to house the labourers working on the tunnelling. Private landlords, of whom there were a great many, let properties at prices which they knew people could afford. Very often the rents were 'inclusive'. That is to say that the landlord accepted responsibility for payment of the rates to the local Council, and he included that cost in the rent. The rates also contained a modest charge for the water supply. So long as tenants paid the rent regularly, their accommodation was secure. The landlord or his representative called round once a week to collect the rent, and it was not unknown for him to bring a small gift for the family at Christmas if they were long-standing tenants.

Rented flats in Mount Pleasant Road.

At the other end of the social scale, all-electric furnished luxury flats were available for rent in the newly-constructed Marine Court, St Leonards-on-Sea. The foundation stone was laid on 30th November 1936, and the whole edifice was built to resemble an ocean liner. It stood 14 stories high and was the very last word in design. One result of the erection of such a tall building was that a resident of East Ascent, whose property lay in its shadow, successfully sued the owners, for loss of light to his premises, and was awarded £250. The rents varied according to

Luxury flats at Marine Court.

the size of the accommodation, but the very cheapest (a one-roomed studio flat) cost £95 per year. The intention was to attract the well-to-do, and hall porters, maids and valets were available on request via a free internal telephone system. The temperature of the whole building was thermostatically controlled winter and summer, and meals could be ordered from a restaurant which had a separate entrance for non-residents. Guest rooms were available when needed for residents' visitors. For those keen on sea-bathing there were underground tunnels giving direct access to the beach.

However, such luxurious surroundings were not for the majority of townspeople. Newly-built semi-detached houses were selling in the thirties for £560, and some people in regular work chose to buy one if they could raise a deposit of £30, and could see far enough ahead to meet the mortgage repayments. For many though, a debt of any kind was unacceptable, and they felt safer renting within their means from week to week. In 1935 such a house in Parker Road could be rented for £1.2.6d per week (£1.12^1/$_2$p) inclusive. Households were run on fairly predictable lines. Mothers seldom went out to work and were therefore 'free' to spend all their time on running the home. There was no provision for school meals and, almost without exception, primary school children came home for a mid-day meal. They were able to do this as the schools were close

'House for Sale' advertisement 1936.

at hand, smaller and more numerous than those of today, so that the children could easily walk to and fro. Many people still regret the loss of the small primary schools of Halton*, Mount Pleasant, All Saints', Cavendish Place, St Andrews, Christ Church, Mercatoria, West St Leonards and St. Matthews*.

With few exceptions all meals were prepared at home. Families seldom went out to a restaurant as this would have been beyond their means, although the occasional treat of fish and chips was brought in, perhaps on a Saturday. Sunday lunch was the best meal of the week when, usually, there was a roast joint of some kind. On Mondays, when the whole morning was spent doing the washing, cooking time was limited. The meal consisted of cold cuts from the Sunday joint served with pickle and quickly prepared 'bubble and squeak' made from the left-over vegetables. If the joint had been

---

* Bombed during the Second World War.

large enough, what remained would be minced to make Tuesday's meal of shepherd's pie or rissoles. The other days brought simple but nourishing home-made dishes of rabbit pie, meat pudding, sausage and mash, beef stew, or liver and onions. The mothers of those days had never heard the expression 'convenience foods' and were very skilled at making the limited house-keeping money go a long way.

One might think that with all those meals to prepare, the shopping would have been a back-breaking task. This was not so. The customer had only to drop a list into the shop, and most large grocers like the World Stores, would deliver the week's groceries by van to the door. The baker and milkman called every day with fresh supplies, and most local butchers and greengrocers had errand boys with delivery bicycles, with a huge basket on the front, to bring the goods to the house. In addition, street traders would call round, usually once a week, selling fish, watercress, or shrimps from a handcart. There was even an elderly man who pushed an old pram containing hearth stone and slabs of pipe clay. These were used for whitening door-steps and the hearth around the ubiquitous kitchen range. This latter piece of household equipment formed, in most homes, the focal point of family life. It ran on coal and was the poor man's Aga. It

Grocery prices in 1936.

provided warmth, a means of cooking meals, heating water and boiling a quick kettle. In the absence of a bathroom, many a child was bathed in a metal tub, in front of such a stove, on a Saturday evening in preparation for Sunday School the next day. If the godliness of the child was in doubt, at least its cleanliness was guaranteed.

The weekly wash was a major undertaking. In the kitchen or scullery there was a brick copper built on a hearth, and housing a water tank shaped like a huge pudding basin. This would be filled with cold water and a fire lit underneath. When the water boiled, soap powder would be added and the sheets and white shirts boiled up and given an occasional stir with a wooden 'copper stick'. Rinsing would be done in the sink, the items 'blued' and starched if necessary, and then wrung out using a mangle with large wooden rollers. This last operation required considerable strength and was very tiring. The hot water would be allowed to cool before being used to wash coloured items by hand. Again, these would be rinsed and put through the mangle, and the whole lot pegged out to dry in the open. The copper would then be baled out into a bucket and the water used to swill and scrub the back yard. Ironing would be done later the same day if possible. For this task, flat-irons were heated on a gas ring or stove, as electric irons had yet to come into common use.

Vacuum cleaners were not widely owned and consequently household cleaning was a tedious and time-consuming job. If there was a carpet, perhaps in the best room, a carpet sweeper would be used. Other floors, usually covered with linoleum, were swept with a soft broom. Any rugs were hung over the line and 'thrashed' with a carpet beater made of woven cane. Kitchen floors were washed daily, and stairs swept down with a dustpan and brush. Doorsteps and kitchen hearths had to be whitened and brass door-knobs and fittings polished regularly.

After all these exhausting chores, and all other considerations aside, mothers were probably too tired to take on work outside the home.

4
EDUCATION

In the years leading up to the Second World War, the children of Hastings and St Leonards were well provided for in matters of education. The town had its own Education Committee under the able direction of Mr W Norman King. Besides the well-run primary and secondary schools, there were open-air schools for delicate children and special schools for children with other needs. The town also had numerous private schools, for boarders and day pupils (See Appendix I). Such establishments brought money to the town, and provided trade for local businesses.

Primary Schools
   It was usual for these schools to have an infant and a junior department, each with its own head teacher, where children were educated from the age of five to eleven. The schools were conveniently placed in every neighbourhood and pupils received six years of solid early grounding in the three R's and other subjects. Schooling was obligatory from the age of five and there were attendance officers quick to ensure that this rule was adhered to. Some schools would take children under five if the parents wished.
   Each pupil was given a third of a pint of milk at playtime each morning, but there was no provision for school meals, as most children went home for their mid-day meal. The only exceptions to this were in areas where some families were very hard-up, and their children went to a nearby soup-kitchen for a meal costing one old penny. Working on the principle of 'mens sana in corpore sano', each child was examined once a year by a visiting doctor, and had their teeth checked by the school dentist. If any treatment was needed the parents were informed. The school nurse also called regularly to look for any signs of scabies or infestations in the hair.
   Female teachers were, with a few exceptions, unmarried, and staff provided a stable environment and an invaluable continuity of teaching. Particular attention was paid to simple arithmetic, and reading and writing skills were honed by daily practice in taking dictation, composition and transcription. In addition to the three R's, children were taught simple handicrafts, given physical education using hoops, skipping ropes and bean-bags, and encouraged to sing and put on little concerts. At morning assembly, one of the first things the little ones learnt was the Lord's Prayer. In the afternoons, any under-five's were made to rest for a while on small camp-beds.
   In the summer of 1935, on the occasion of the Silver Jubilee of King George V and Queen Mary, invitations went out to all primary school

children to attend an afternoon celebration, on the upper lawn, in Alexandra Park. They were entertained by a Punch and Judy show and watched a parade in the form of a costumed pageant, to which each school contributed with a group of children portraying a nursery rhyme. Every child was given a picnic tea in a cardboard cake box, and presented with a commemorative tea-spoon supplied by the Mayor, Alderman Arthur Blackman.

Spoon presented to school pupils by the Mayor to commemorate the Royal Silver Jubilee in 1935.

At the age of seven plus, children moved from the infant to the junior school, where teaching continued on much the same lines, except that the classes were arranged according to aptitude. The time-table included lessons in geography, history, current affairs, sewing or wood-work, games, and swimming sessions at the White Rock Baths. Arithmetic lessons were intensified and by the age of ten, tables had been systematically learnt by rote, and children were doing long division, simple square roots, decimals, fractions and practising mental arithmetic. In addition to these skills, they learnt to measure in centimetres, and to calculate in pounds, shillings and pence, feet and inches, pints and gallons and even pecks and bushels. Discipline was strict. Pupils were not expected to talk to one another in class, and were made to stand behind the blackboard or in the corridor if they transgressed. If any really severe offences were committed, perhaps by boys fighting in the playground, punishment was by caning. The cane was kept tucked away in the Head's office but its presence was widely known, and bad behaviour carefully avoided by the majority of pupils. All canings had to be recorded in a punishment book.

The pupils' progress was regularly checked at least once a year through tests. Marks were awarded and children and parents told of the results. In the Spring of their last year at junior school, all children sat the scholarship examination - later to be called the 'eleven plus'. This consisted of a morning spent in a nearby secondary school answering written questions on the three R's and general knowledge, and taking an IQ test. Later in the year, the results were made known and, according to how well they had done in the examination, the children were allocated to the various secondary schools in the Borough. If any parent felt their child had been wrongly placed, there was a possiblity of taking the examination again at the age of twelve.

Secondary Schools

Those who had gained very good marks in the examination were offered scholarships at either the Hastings Boys' Grammar School in Nelson Road, or

The Old Grammar School in Nelson Road.

the Hastings High School for Girls on The Ridge. These schools were both fee-paying. They were staffed by graduates, and offered an academic style of education which could lead on to a university place with prospects of professional work at the end of it all. Parents, who accepted such places for their children, were means tested with the result that some were asked to pay part or all of the fees, which, in the case of the High School, were £12 per year. They were also asked to sign an undertaking that their child, 'shall follow the prescribed course of study up to the end of the school year in which the pupil attains the age of 16 years, and to pay the sum of £5 in the event of such pupil being withdrawn'. (The official leaving age was, at that time, 14). School uniform was required to be worn and for poorer families there were grants to help with the cost. For many children, attendance at these schools meant quite a long journey to school. A free bus pass was given to those who lived over a certain distance away, and the rest were expected to walk, cycle, or pay their own fares.

Children with somewhat lower marks were allocated to one of the excellent Central Schools, either at Priory Road where boys and girls were taught in separate schools, or to Tower Road in St Leonards which was mixed. From the Central Schools, many of the pupils left to take jobs in shops, offices, banks and other 'white collar' posts. Some chose to

HASTINGS GRAMMAR SCHOOL FOUNDATION

The Hastings Grammar School, founded in 1619 by William Parker, was re-organised in 1878 by the Charity Commissioners. It has grown considerably since then, until in 1938 there were 405 boys in the School

Recently the Governors have approved plans for New Buildings to accommodate 520. There is a Preparatory Department for young boys, as well as a Boarding House, over both of which the Governors have control

There are twenty Scholarships tenable at the School, and four Leaving Scholarships

The School is on the list of efficient Secondary Schools, and is inspected from time to time by the Board of Education

For details of fees, etc., application should be made to the Headmaster, Mr. M. G. G. Hyder, M.A., B.Sc. (Oxon) or to the Clerk to the Governors, Westminster Bank Chambers, Hastings

Grammar School advertisement in 1939.

attend evening classes to acquire secretarial skills or to learn accountancy in order to better their prospects.

The remainder went to one of the Senior or Technical Schools where emphasis was on practical and manual skills. The boys learnt woodwork and metalwork, while the girls were taught laundrywork, domestic skills and cooking. Many of these children went on, at the age of fourteen, to become apprentices in a trade of some sort, and to secure steady jobs in due course.

In the secondary schools, discipline continued to be strict, particularly at the Grammar and High Schools. The boys were given lines, detention or 15 minutes PD (punishment drill) out-of-doors. In some cases they were made to memorise lines of poetry, or were deprived of a merit half-day holiday. For a really bad offence there was a 'swishing' with the cane. There was no *'creeping like a snail, unwillingly to school'*, as good attendance and punctuality were expected at all times.

Hastings Central School in Priory Road.

At the High School, emphasis was very much on 'lady-like' comportment. Best behaviour was expected at all times, especially when in school uniform outside the school. Pupils were instructed not to eat in the street, and at least one girl was admonished for being seen licking an ice-cream cone in public. The subjects offered under inclusive fees were shown as follows in the 1938 Prospectus:

CURRICULUM.

The subjects of instruction under inclusive fees are :—

Religious Knowledge.	French.
English Language, Literature, etc.	Latin.
English and European History.	Drawing.
Geography.	Needlework.
Mathematics.	Music.
Science (Biology, Physics, General Elementary Science and Nature Study).	Physical Training and Games.
Commercial Subjects.	

The Governors aimed *'to provide for girls a course of instruction in the subjects necessary to a good general education, upon the lines suitable for scholars from 9 to 19 years of age.'*

When a mistress entered a classroom at the start of a lesson, the girls were asked to show due respect by standing up. In the school dining-room, staff sat on a platform. Any unnecessary talking by the girls drew immediate attention, and miscreants were made to stand and be reprimanded.

In both the Grammar and High Schools, the ultimate punishment was expulsion. This was a very rare occurrence as, apart from the disgrace, the scholarship was forfeited. The prospectus also states, *'The Governors may at any time, without giving notice or cause, dismiss any pupil for idleness, disobedience, or other serious misconduct, or for irregularity of attendance, after having given the pupil or her parents an opportunity of making any explanation or excuses'.*

Although selection by examination was by no means a perfect system for deciding to which secondary school a child was sent, by and large it worked reasonably well and had much to recommend it. Those who went to the Senior or Technical Schools could be sure that besides continuing to receive a good basic education, pupils' practical and manual talents would be given every chance to develop. Pupils at the Central Schools had the advantage of being educated among their intellectual peers and within their capabilities. Given the secondary education system then in vogue, those who were offered scholarships were set on the road to higher education, and this represented the only such chance poorer children were ever likely to get.

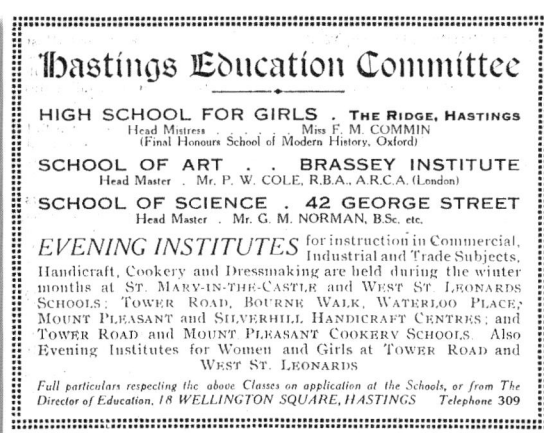

Hastings Education Committee's advertisement.

5
TRANSPORT AND TRAVEL

Could the people of today walk to work, without undue hardship? The very question would cause hands to be raised in horror. That, however, was exactly what they did in Hastings in the days preceding the 2nd World War.

In those days, the town was much more compact in terms of housing. The big council estates of Churchill Avenue and Malvern Way had yet to be built. The Hollington estate was much smaller, and the Ashford Road and Parkstone Road developments were still farmland. The land which the Conquest Hospital now occupies together with its surrounding housing, belonged to Little Ridge Farm, and the Elphinstone School site and much of Parker Road were part of Blacklands Farm.

Although bus and trolley-bus services were frequent, reliable and fairly cheap, they were used sparingly. Except in wet weather, the townsfolk, given the hilly nature of the town, would walk downhill and take the bus for the return journey, thus saving their pennies for other things. Advertisements of the time seem to indicate that more custom was being sought.

The trolley-bus network, which was clean and silent, covered the greater part of the town and extended as far as Cooden to the west of Bexhill. In 1935 Maidstone & District Motor Services, which had operated long distance routes into Hastings for many years, took over the running of the trolley-buses from The Hastings Tramways Company.

The steep Castle Hill Road, leading to the West Hill and beyond, had never been wired for trolley-buses and had its own motor bus service. As the town grew, more motor-buses were introduced to serve the new Parker Road and the upper part of St Helen's Road.

Traffic on the roads, which by today's standards would have been considered fairly light, consisted largely of buses and trolley-buses, delivery vans and

Trolley buses at the memorial prior to WW2.
(Photo: L. Rowe collection)

lorries, motorcycle combinations and bicycles. The few taxis already in existence, were increased in the late thirties by a new firm. This was the Grey Car Company with its much acclaimed '6d per mile' and its drivers in smart uniforms. It operated mainly from the railway stations for the benefit of holiday-makers and their luggage. On the whole local people rarely used taxis, except in an emergency or late at night.

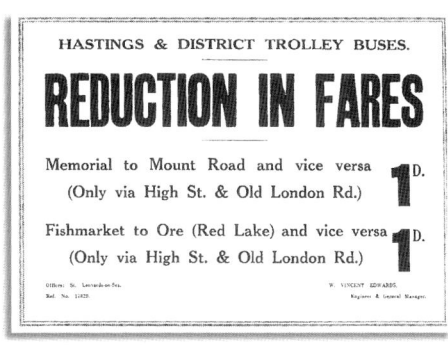

Fares reduced in the 1930s.

Private cars formed only a minor part of the local traffic as they were beyond the means of most people. Those that were seen on the roads were mainly owned by local professional and business people, or belonged to better-off visitors to the town. Until the late thirties, even the local police had to make do with just two motorcycle combinations.

However, it was anticipated that private car ownership would increase. Mr Sidney Little, the far-sighted Borough Engineer of the time, introduced new underground car-parks which were opened in 1931 and are still used today. He also recognised that the congestion in the narrow main road through the Old Town (High Street) would need to be relieved. In 1935 he formulated a carefully-costed scheme which he presented to the Town Council. This was for a new road to be cut through the area, running from Marine Parade, crossing George Street to the foot of the West Hill lift, over Exmouth Place and the Croft, to join up with Old London Road through Tor Field. Despite considerable public opposition, the

Advertisement for a new car in the 1930s.

proposal was eventually approved by the full Council. For various reasons the work was delayed and soon after the beginning of the second World War, Mr Little was seconded to work for the Admiralty, and his plan was never carried out.

The summer season brought great numbers of day-trippers from London and elsewhere. They would all arrive during the morning by coach looking pale-faced. The coaches dropped their passengers off before parking for a few hours in the Old Town. Whilst in the town, the visitors enjoyed a day on the beach, or sampling the local fish and chips and pubs - very much as they do today. In the early evening, the passengers would return to their coaches having, in the meantime, become startlingly red of face from exposure to sea air and sun. They were all gone again by 6 o'clock, as that was the local requirement. This popular use of coaches kept Hastings town centre clear of traffic and fumes throughout the day. Special excursion trains also brought large groups of visitors from the capital and elsewhere in much the same way.

For residents of Hastings who needed to travel out of town, either for business or pleasure, there was a good steam train service provided by Southern Railway. In 1935 the line running westwards out of Ore station was electrified and the first such train was seen in Hastings on 5th May. Tickets were affordable and the company advertised excursions to many places in the South East and London. A day could be spent in Brighton for 3/2d (16p), in Folkestone or Canterbury for 4/2d (21p), whilst a day in London could be had for 6/3d (31p). If anyone had 15/3d (76p) to buy an inclusive train/boat ticket, three hours could be spent ashore in Dieppe.

A day out with Southern Railway.

During the summer season, the more adventurous who wanted to take to the water from Hastings Pier, would find one of P & A Campbell's paddle steamers ready and willing to oblige. At high tide passengers embarked from the landing stage at the far end of the pier (now, alas, rotted away). Once on board, travellers could go below to look through a window into the engine room, where the huge shafts were working hard to turn the paddles. The sound they made as they slapped their way across the channel was unforgettable. Several of the steamers, including 'The Brighton Belle', were destined to meet a sad end at Dunkirk. Two shillings (10p) would buy a ticket to spend an hour or two in Brighton, whilst ten shillings and sixpence (52$^1/_2$p) would take you all the way to Boulogne for a jolly day spent sampling the French delights.

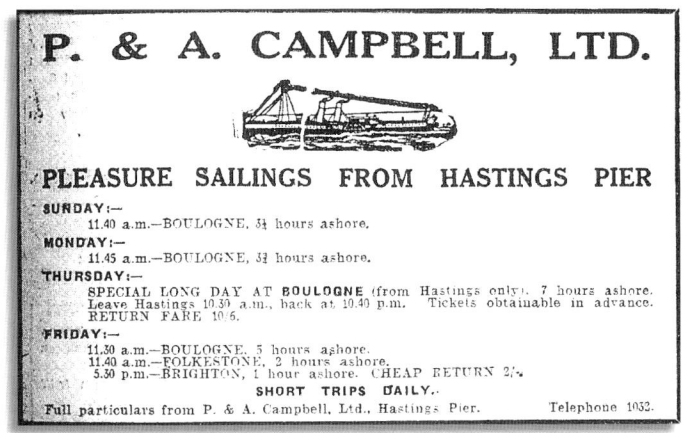

A trip to France for 10/6d (52p).

6
LEISURE AND PLEASURE

The Bandstand at Hastings Pier.

One of the advantages of living in a seaside resort was that the amenities, and summer-time attractions provided for holiday-makers, were also available to the permanent residents if they wished. Hastings in the thirties was no exception. Many of the pleasures cost very little and some were even free. A pleasant summer-time stroll along the 'prom' on a fine summer evening was enlivened by the band playing on the Pier. Deck-chairs surrounding the band-stand were available for a few pence, while passers-by could pause for a few minutes to enjoy the music. A similar scene took place on Sunday afternoons at the Alexandra Park bandstand, where chairs cost 3d and Albert Davison and his band played. Joseph Hay handed out song-sheets and encouraged everyone to sing. Children, and others who did not have 3d, could sit on the grass and join in anyway. After a pleasant hour or two spent in that way, the audience was ready for some refreshment at the nearby tea-room.

At the White Rock Pavilion, built principally as a concert hall and opened by the Prince of Wales in 1927, the Hastings Municipal Orchestra put on some fine winter concerts under the direction of Julius Harrison. The summer season saw the arrival of the 'Fol-de-Rols, and other popular variety shows. Tea-dances were held every weekday afternoon and cost 1/6 (7^{1}/$_{2}$p), including tea. Across the road on Hastings pier, the Court Players held their season of weekly plays from September to June in the cosy repertory theatre.

The New Palace Pier at St Leonards, sadly destroyed by fire after World War 2, was the venue for those whose tastes were for the 'café chantant' or wrestling matches. Ballroom dancers were also provided for. In 1938, for instance, a 'Grand Ball' was advertised at an admission price of 1/6 (7^1/$_2$p).

Cinemas, of which there were at least seven, provided perhaps the most popular form of pre-war entertainment. They were, the Kinema in Norman Road, the Elite and the Regal – both near Warrior Square Station, and the Silverhill Picture House (now a carpet shop) in St Leonards. Hastings had the Plaza in Cambridge Road, the Cinema de Luxe (now a Bingo Hall), and the Gaiety - the only remaining present-day cinema – opposite the Town Hall. The Cinema de Luxe had once been a theatre and on Saturday mornings, 4d would buy a child's ticket for a seat in the 'gods'. This meant a climb up endless stairs to seats which were just wooden planks. There, they would see an exciting serial film, which always ended on a cliff-hanger, so as to ensure an audience for the following week.

On 19th March 1938 a splendid new cinema, the Ritz, was opened by the Mayor on the site of the present-day ESK warehouse in Cambridge Road. Said to cost £100,000, the work was carried out to the highest standards of comfort and safety, and reached near-perfection in matters of seating, acoustics and vision. It opened with the feature film 'Maria Walewska' starring Clark Gable and Greta Garbo. In the interval between films, while usherettes served ice-creams, a magnificent £10,000 Wurlitzer organ, lit from within by changing coloured lights, would rise up through the floor bearing aloft the organist, Mr Wilfred Southworth. The audience would then enjoy a mini-concert of popular tunes, before settling down to the watch the supporting film. Ticket prices ranged from 6d to 2/- (2^1/$_2$p to 10p in decimal currency), and included free car-parking. To complete the luxurious surroundings, there was a well equipped café on the first floor with seating for 170 people.

For people with more of a taste for physical activities, Hastings offered two 18-hole golf courses. Tennis courts and bowling greens were available in Alexandra Park and White Rock Gardens. Swimmers not only had

---

Telephone : Hastings 2068 & 2067

Hastings Bathing Pool
— and —
Winter Sports Centre
Manager : Commander J. Drinkwater, R.N. (Retd.)

SUMMER	WINTER
Swimming, Diving and Sun Bathing. Physical Drill, Deck Games and Squash Rackets	Roller Skating, Squash Rackets, Table Tennis, Fencing and Boxing, etc.

COMPETENT INSTRUCTORS IN ATTENDANCE

Bathing Pool attractions in the 1930s.

Air Display in 1936.

Circus and Fair at Summerfields in 1936.

sea-bathing along the whole of the extensive beaches, but the White Rock Baths offered a choice of two heated pools as well as sea water, medicated and Turkish baths and massage. The sheltered, open-air Bathing Pool at St Leonards also offered squash courts, cafés and an upper terrace for roller skating.

For the less energetic, a stroll along the 'prom' was possible even in wet weather as it was, and still is, in two tiers between Hastings Pier and Warrior Square. The lower one was nick-named 'Bottle Alley' because of the attractive mosaics of thousands of coloured glass pieces set into the wall. The seaward side could be entirely enclosed in bad weather by sliding glass windows, set into metal runners. Unfortunately these were not used very often and they became corroded and eventually fell into disuse. If the stroll was extended beyond Warrior Square, one would arrive at the Sun Lounge (now the Marine Pavilion). This was a fine venue for refreshments, concerts, and tea-dances.

If anyone fancied a sea trip, there were short boat rides from the beach for 1/- (5p), or a hair-raising ride in a speed-boat from the pier.

A rare treat was provided for everyone in July 1936 when C W A Scott's Air Display arrived at Church Farm, Fairlight. It took place on Friday July 31st, and gave three complete displays at intervals throughout the day. No doubt inspired by Amy Johnson's recent exploits as the famous English woman aviator, crowds flocked to the site high up on the cliffs at Fairlight overlooking the sea. As well as watching the displays they could, if they had 3/6d (17^{1}/$_{2}$p) to spare, experience the thrill of a short 'flip' in one of the planes. It was a day to remember.

Local children (of all ages) knew how to find entertainment for very little outlay. There was the Carnival procession each summer which cost nothing to watch. In the same week a travelling fair and circus arrived at Summerfields on the site of the present Sports Centre. Even if pocket money was short, fun could be had watching contestants wielding a sledgehammer, whilst vying to ring the bell on the 'Try your Strength' machine. Alternatively, a crafty peep into the boxing tent revealed pugilistic scenes of aggression where anyone, who wanted to try his luck, was invited to have a few rounds with a trained boxer.

Another free spectacle was to be found at low tide. At the end of Robertson Street a stretch of shore, devoid of shingle, presented a large area of flat damp sand. There, using a stick, a sand-artist would draw grand pictures of churches and castles to the wonderment of all who saw him. He earned a little money from the pennies thrown down by the spectators, and it was very sad, later in the day, to see the tide come in and wash all his efforts away.

Biddy the Tubman also entertained young and old alike with his aquatic tricks in his old wooden tub, while a helper on the beach passed the hat round.

The boating lake in Alexandra Park provided great pleasure for youngsters. For a 6d half-hour ticket, there was choice of rowing boats, tiny paddle boats for the little ones, or canoes for those with 'Grey Owl' ambitions. Once embarked on the lake, the children's enjoyment was only interrupted by the dreaded cry of, 'Come in Number 6, your time is up'.

The Boating Lake in Alexandra Park. War Memorial can be seen in background.

As well as the adult attractions already mentioned on the New Palace Pier at St Leonards, children were also drawn there to the many side-shows. 'Professor' E Bradley Warren, one of the showmen, ran a performing troupe. One Sunday evening in July 1936 there was a sad occurrence during a heavy thunderstorm, when one of his performers was killed by lightning. The other showmen organised a whip-round and a special coffin was built for the deceased. At the funeral, Chopin's Funeral March was played, followed by the Last Post, and wreaths were received from pier staff in loving memory of the late lamented who was - 'Bonzo' the performing flea.

At home, pleasures for children were of a simple kind. They amused themselves with pastimes such as Snakes and Ladders, Ludo, Draughts, Tiddlywinks, and simple card games. Some children had a few clockwork toys or a magic lantern, but there were no electronic toys of any kind. At school, children had their own playground games. The girls skipped, played hopscotch, 'Mr Wolf' or, at the right season, brought out their whips and tops. The boys had their traditional marbles, 'fag'-cards, and five-stones. A favourite boys' game in winter was 'sliding'. This was done in hobnailed boots until a strip of playground which gradually became longer, acquired a polished, glass-like surface.

Television, which was in its infancy, started from Alexandra Palace in November 1936. In February 1938, in an attempt to see whether TV could be received in Hastings, a successful experiment was carried out at Hydneye House School on the Ridge. That appears to have been the only time TV was seen in the town before the war. Such broadcasts as there were elsewhere, had a limited duration and range. At that time, it was estimated that only about 20,000 television sets existed in the whole country.

On the other hand radio, or wireless as it was then known, provided widespread pleasure to young and old alike. Children would come home from school for tea and their daily treat of Children's Hour. The programme included a variety of interesting items. There were serialised readings of books such as 'Swallows and Amazons', whilst Toy Town stories were always great favourites with the younger children. Commander Stephen King Hall and the Zoo Man both gave most interesting talks pitched at just the right level for the young listeners. At the end of the programme, just before the news at 6 o'clock, the much-loved Uncle Mac would bid them all, *'Good night children'*.

7
GATHERING CLOUDS

Throughout the 1930's, the people of Hastings were living their normal lives, earning a living, bringing up their children, enjoying their surroundings and experiencing all the usual joys and sorrows that life brought them. The rhythm of the years followed an established pattern. Summer visitors came and went, followed by the winter semi-hibernation of the town. School terms began and ended. However, there were some activities taking place, in Hastings and elsewhere, that were not part of normal life, and which gave rise to a growing sense of unease.

Adolf Hitler, founder and leader of Germany's Nazi Party, became German Chancellor in 1933, having initially gained power in a free election. With his compelling powers of oratory, he quickly received mass support for his condemnation of the Jews and Communists. He had visions of restoring German greatness in Europe and rapidly took control of the country's political and economic institutions, crushing all opposition.

Cinemas in Hastings screened newsreels of Hitler's speeches to rallies of the German people. The fervent way in which he addressed his massed audiences as he announced his plans for an all-conquering Nazi 'master race', inspired the German people to follow his lead. In 1936, while the rest of the world looked on in disbelief, he flagrantly breached international treaties in carrying out an unopposed annexation of the Rhineland. A wide-ranging programme of re-armament had been set in place in 1935, which broke the treaty of Versailles, and by September 1937, Hitler was watching manoeuvres of his armed forces at Mecklenberg. In Germany's big cities, air-raid precautions were being rehearsed, and black-out arrangements practised. In short, Hitler was preparing for war. He then embarked on a programme of aggressive expansion in pursuit of his aims. In 1938 his armies marched into Austria and incorporated it into the 3rd Reich. He next laid claim to the Sudetenland (part of Czechoslovakia), whilst, at the same time, casting acquisitive eyes over other European countries. His ambitions to conquer the whole of Europe were becoming clear, and causing alarm in Britain and the rest of the continent. In 1938, in an attempt to appease Hitler and curb his ambition, an agreement was signed at Munich between Britain, France, Germany and her ally, Italy. Under this, the Sudetenland would be taken from Czechoslovakia and given to Germany. It was understood that Hitler would make no further claims. Newsreels were shown of Britain's Prime Minister, Neville Chamberlain, arriving back by plane, waving the now famous 'piece of paper' and confidently declaring, 'I believe it is peace in our time'. His confidence was misplaced: Hitler was not to be trusted. Six months later, in

March 1939, armies of German troops overran and occupied the whole of Czechoslovakia.

Whilst all these events were taking place, Hastings, together with the rest of Britain, was being urged by the government to make its own preparations for war.

As early as 1936, gas masks costing 7/6d (37½p) were being offered for sale in the Hastings Observer, and former stables at Bo-Peep were converted into an ARP training centre. In November of the same year, police officers and firemen attended a week-long course on anti-gas measures. This was followed by training in air-raid precautions. Early in 1937 a call went out for 80-90 volunteers for the Auxiliary Fire Service. An appeal for 500 Air Raid Wardens followed. In September, Boots the chemist in Robertson St displayed a 'gas-proof' room and in the same month a demonstration was held at Summerfields on how to deal with incendiary bombs.

In the autumn term of 1938, the Boys at the Grammar School in Nelson Road dug trenches in the grounds and sandbagged 'the arches' for protection. In the same year there was a free distribution of gas masks to the general public from the Central Hall at Bank Buildings and other centres around the town. Three sizes of mask were available and boy scouts were called upon to help with the fitting and disinfecting of specimen masks. Thousands of cardboard boxes to keep them in followed shortly afterwards. A call again went out for more Air Raid Wardens as it was estimated that a total of 1,100 would be needed.

Sandbagging 'The Arches' at the Boys' Grammar School.

In January 1939, the Local Authority received a request from the Ministry of Health for facilities and accommodation to be made available in the town for

Digging trenches at the Boys' Grammar School.

evacuees from danger areas. Billeting allowances were to be 10/6d (52½p) for one child and 8/6d (42½p) each for two or more. Mothers alone were to receive 5/- (25p) towards lodgings.

As the year progressed, so the preparations for war accelerated. A Police War Duties Department was set up consisting of a small group of officers with responsibility for co-ordinating Air Raid Precautions. One senior officer, who had seen earlier service in the Royal Artillery, was sent, first to the Home Office School for ARP Officers, and later to the Army Bomb Reconnaissance Course at Tunbridge Wells. He thereby became qualified for the hazardous job of investigating, identifying and reporting all unexploded bombs and other missiles which were, eventually, to fall on Hastings. He was, after the war began, to have an extra task on one occasion of removing a mentally disturbed woman from the uncharted minefield which had been sown by Canadian troops at Ecclesbourne Glen. She lived in one of the old Coast Guard cottages on the slope overlooking the glen (now eroded away) and was found sitting on the bridge inside the mined area reading the family Bible. With the help of a colleague, he managed to persuade her to come out, fearing all the while that one of the mines would explode.

Bomb Reconnaissance Armband issued to certain Police Officers.

By April, air-raid shelters were on offer to the general public for between £10 and £15, whilst new houses in Harold Road came already equipped with one. Boy scouts were kept busy filling sandbags for use against bomb-blast elsewhere. The large basement cloakroom at the Girls' High School, which was to serve as a shelter, had a wall of sandbags placed outside the windows. A number of covered trenches appeared at Torfield as public refuges, remains of which can still be seen today. Basements and the underground car parks were designated as public shelters. In addition, the general population was advised how best to protect themselves in their own homes.

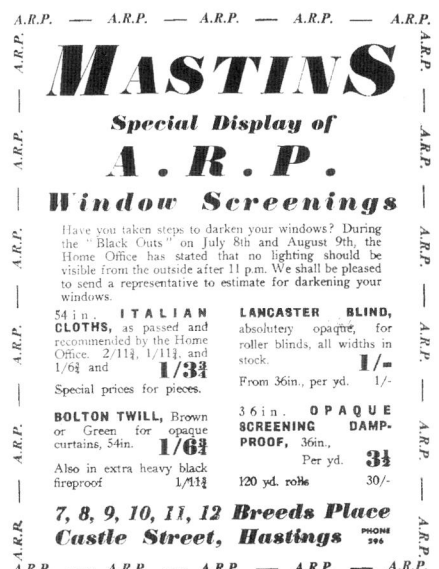

Materials on sale for trial blackout planned for July 1939.

In May, plans were completed to receive up to 11,000 evacuees from London, which would have greatly increased the population. In June compulsory military training was introduced. The first 'call-up' day saw 240 local young men registering at the Employment Exchange in Priory Street. In the same month we learnt that a trial black-out would take place, covering the whole of Kent and Sussex, from 11pm to 4am on the night of 8/9th July. Its start was signalled by fire sirens supplemented by steam whistles and hooters from various laundries and factories. Kerb edges were painted white and hoods placed on traffic lights. All street lamps were extinguished, and people and traffic were advised to move with extreme caution. This gave rise to strong criticism from representatives of the tourist industry over a wide area, who thought it inappropriate and damaging to the trade of holiday resorts.

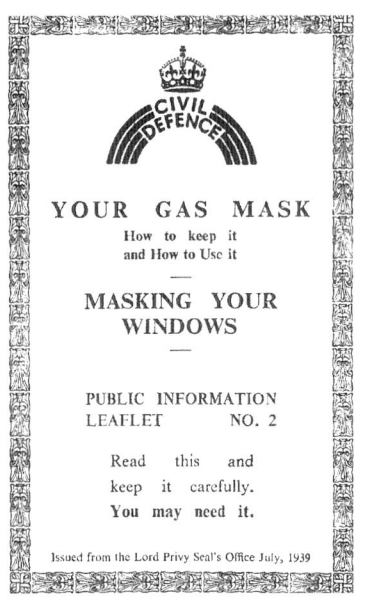

Advice leaflet on Gas Masks and Blackout.

July also brought an appeal for volunteers to join the Women's Land Army. These were intended to replace male agricultural workers called to military service. In the same month a leaflet was issued telling us, 'How to keep and use your gas mask', but although the distribution had been well publicised, by August 1939, 11,000 masks remained unclaimed. The same leaflet carried instructions on how to mask windows, and householders began to make thick blinds or screens to ensure that no lights were visible from outside. There was a second black-out exercise on August 10th.

Parliament was recalled. Both Houses met on August 24th when the 'Emergency Powers (Defence) Act 1939' was immediately passed.

Whilst all these preparations were in progress, an exceptionally fine summer brought crowds of seemingly care-free holiday-makers to the town. As late as August 27th, Southern Railway was advertising a day trip to Dieppe (no passports required for British subjects), for around 75p. P & A Campbell's paddle steamer 'The Brighton Queen' carried on making its customary trips from Hastings Pier to Boulogne, and tourist attractions were in full swing. Bertram Mills' Circus spent the last week of the month at South Saxons fields, and local children were enjoying what was to be their last peace-time school holiday for many years. At the same time, their parents were being advised to stock up with tinned food, to assemble first-aid kits and fire-fighting gear, and to get to know the local air-raid warden. Those last few days of peace, were lived in a truly strange world made up of many incongruous elements.

On 31st August, the government issued orders for the evacuation of London, and other large cities, to begin the next day. Strangely optimistic, the BBC 1 o'clock news on that day warned that *'no one should assume that this decision means war is inevitable'*.

On 1st September 1939, in blatant disregard of all undertakings, Hitler's armies invaded Poland thus giving rise to urgent diplomatic activity between London and Berlin.

All street lighting was switched off, and black-out restrictions imposed immediately. Over the three days from 1st to 3rd September, 3,000 evacuee children arrived in Hastings from the London area. Another 180 hospital stretcher cases arrived, and were dispersed to local hospitals. In all, 4,500 were eventually accommodated in the town. Frank Ashworth, the son of a local bank manager recently moved into the town, recalls that his mother had an unexpected visit from the billeting officer. He told her that the previous occupants of the house had offered to take four children. Having two children of her own, she kindly agreed to take two little girls from Deptford who screamed at the sight of, what must have been, their first bath. On the whole though, most of the evacuees coped very well with the upheaval in their lives. They arrived in the town bringing with them just what they could carry in a small case or parcel plus, of course, the ubiquitous gas mask. The local authority's plans for this event had been carefully rehearsed, and fell smoothly put into place. One hundred tons of food stuffs had arrived at Hastings Station and been transferred to the underground car-park at Harold Place. The arriving children walked in orderly lines from the trains to the car-park where trestle tables had been set up. Teams of local government officials issued them all with a carrier bag of food and then allocated them to their billets. With the influx of these unusual late summer visitors, Hastings saw its last peace-time holiday season draw to a close.

Last trips to Dieppe before outbreak of WW2.

On Saturday September 2nd (the eve of war), in an atmosphere strangely evocative of the sinking of the Titanic, the band of the 10th Royal Hussars played in the bandstand on the pier, which, unlike the rest of the town, remained brilliantly illuminated.

8
SUNDAY, 3rd SEPTEMBER 1939

The day broke bright and fine in Hastings, and bore no early indication that it was to be anything but a normal Sunday. Churchgoers may have murmured an extra prayer or two that the war clouds, which had been gathering for so long might, miraculously, disperse, but most people went about their usual business - there was no reason to do otherwise. A ten-year-old schoolgirl of the time recalls, *'I set off as usual for Sunday School at Blacklands Church just before ten o'clock. On that morning, it seems there had been a radio announcement saying that the Prime Minister was to address the nation at 11.15am. I arrived home shortly after eleven o'clock to find my mother tuning the radio. She told me the Prime Minister was about to speak, and I was to sit down with her and listen. We heard Neville Chamberlain's thin cultured voice uttering his never-to-be-forgotten words, "I am speaking to you from the Cabinet Room at 10, Downing Street. This morning the British Ambassador in Berlin handed the German Government a final Note stating that, unless we heard from them by 11 o'clock that they were prepared at once to withdraw their troops from Poland, a state of war would exist between us. I have to tell you that no such undertaking has been received, and that consequently this country is at war with Germany".* His words reduced my mother to silent tears as she sat ashen-faced listening intently. He went on to say, "Now may God bless you all and may He defend the right. For it is evil things that we shall be fighting against, brute force, bad faith, injustice, oppression and persecution. And against them I am certain

> ## THE AIR RAID WARNING
>
> Warnings of impending air raids will be given by a fluctuating or "warbling" signal of varying pitch, or a succession of intermittent blasts sounded by hooters and sirens.
>
> These signals may be supplemented by sharp blasts on police whistles.
>
> The " Raiders Passed " signal will be a continuous signal at a steady pitch.
>
> If poison gas has been used warning will be given by hand rattles.
>
> The ringing of handbells will announce that the danger from gas has passed.

Air Raid Warning notice published by Hastings and St Leonards Observer on 2nd September, 1939.

that the right will prevail." Within a few minutes the air-raid sirens sounded and we waited fearfully, hearts thumping, expecting an immediate air attack, but nothing happened. Around noon the 'raiders past' sounded'.

In the afternoon, a BBC news bulletin announced that the air raid warning had been a false alarm. It also said that all places of entertainment were to be closed until further notice. The announcer went on to advise everyone to keep off the streets as much as possible, to carry their gas masks everywhere, and to make sure everyone had their name and address clearly written on a luggage label or envelope and to keep it on them always.

That evening at 6 o'clock, King George VI spoke to the nation. He referred to *'this grave hour'* and went on to call on *'my people at home and my peoples across the seas . . . to stand firm and united in this time of trial'.*

Later news bulletins said that France too, was at war with Germany, and that Australia had also joined in. We also heard that from the following day petrol would cost 1/6d a gallon (7$\frac{1}{2}$p) and would be of one grade only called 'Pool'. Such limited-range television programmes as there were at that time, ceased abruptly on that day, and the 20,000 screens in Britain were to remain blank for many years.

From then on, the household radio set became a vital means of communication, a kind of umbilical cord whereby the government, through the BBC, supplied us with all kinds of information, instructions, warnings and advice concerning our daily lives. It became almost a duty to listen every day and so keep up-to-date, not only with the progress of the war, but to know what we, as a nation, were expected to do, and how we were to behave. Thus began a war that was to change everyone's life, and cast dark shadows over the whole world.

9
THE PHONEY WAR

The next six months came to be known as the 'phoney' war, although there was nothing phoney about the abrupt way Hastings took on its wartime aspect. Air-raid shelters, warden posts, sandbags, windows criss-crossed with sticky tape, men in uniform, and darkened streets became familiar sights. The holiday-makers who had so recently thronged the sea-front had vanished and been replaced by airmen, billeted in Marine Court, doing 'PT on the prom'. Although there was no compulsion to carry one's gas-mask, most people did so, and the cardboard box became a commonplace accessory. Some cinemas imposed a rule that entry was to be barred to those without one. This caused some heated arguments. Our innovative underground car parks of which the town was so proud, suffered the ignominy of being labelled as public shelters as the whole town shifted into war-time mode. Buses stopped running at 9.0 p.m., and milk deliveries were restricted to one a day.

The black-out lasted from sunset to sunrise, and the exact times were published in the local paper. Many injuries were caused as people found it difficult to adapt to the darkness. Hastings was no exception. On 9th September, six days into the war, a man was knocked down and killed by a car in St Leonards. Thereafter, pedestrians were advised to wear or carry something white to aid visibility. Torches were allowed to be carried, but were to have two layers of tissue paper behind the glass. They had to be pointed downwards to indicate the holders' presence when crossing the road, and were not to be used at all during an air-raid warning.

People kept busy with their scissors and needles making covers for their gas-mask boxes, from a simple pattern published in the local newspaper.

On September 18th, the children all went back to school to find themselves, in most cases, sharing the premises with a school from London. At the Hastings High School, as in most other schools, the day was split in two. The local girls used the classrooms for half the day, leaving it to the evacuees from a convent school for the rest of the time. When not in school, the girls had games, swimming lessons at the White Rock Baths, or went for nature walks with a mistress. On some days, church halls were used for other activities.

The British Expeditionary Force had been sent to France, and the troops were seen on newsreels, smiling at the camera, but very little was said of what they were doing at that time.

Petrol rationing started on September 22nd. The basic monthly ration varied according to the size of the car, i.e. four gallons for an Austin 7, eight gallons for a Ford 8, and up to ten gallons for larger cars. These amounts were roughly enough for 100 - 200 miles.

Meanwhile, the courts were being severe with people who failed to observe the black-out regulations. The maximum punishment for infringement was £100 fine, or 3 months imprisonment, or both. On one day at the end of September, the Mayor of Hastings, presiding over the Petty Sessions, imposed fines ranging from £1 to £2 on seven offenders, stating that regulations must be strictly complied with. In spite of his warning, there continued to be regular processions of offenders before the courts.

October proved to be the month when Hastings really began to notice the effects of war-time restrictions, measures, and changes. Early in the month, National Registration took place. Every household received a form on which to enter the names of everyone in the house, including children. Using the information obtained, Identity Cards were issued, with instructions to carry them always and to produce them when required to do so by a member of the police or military. Ration Books for food were issued to everyone, although rationing was not to start until the following January. Parents of evacuee children were asked to contribute 6/- (30p) per week for each

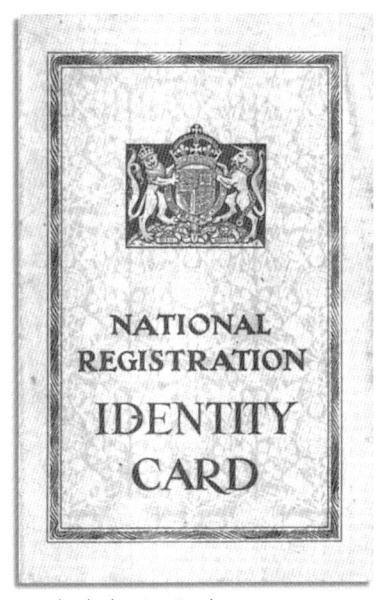

Standard Identity Card.

child, to help offset the cost of the scheme. This led to many parents removing their children from reception areas such as Hastings, and by the end of the year, in spite of the government's advice, on average about 2/5ths of the evacuees had been taken back home to London and other big cities.

The most valuable items in Hastings museum were removed and sent to Wales for safe-keeping.

Sadness came to the town later in October with news of the town's first military casualties. Two local men, AB William John Ford aged 20, and Boy

Albert Card aged 16, were killed at Scapa Flow on HMS Royal Oak.

In the Town Council, questions were asked as to how much money the Council would save on street lighting because of the black-out. The answer was £18,000. It was suggested by the questioner that rate-payers were not getting what they had paid for. The Mayor explained that estimates for lighting had been drawn up months before and that if, because of the circumstances, those costs had been overstated, then other areas of expenditure had been underestimated, thus evening out the figures. Other questions were asked concerning the town's 860 air-raid wardens, of whom 76 were paid (£3 per week for men and £2 for women), whilst the rest received nothing. It was alleged some of those who were paid had private incomes, and did not need the money. Details were requested for the total expenditure. It was revealed that only full-time wardens were paid, and they were those with special responsibilities or in charge of a group. In answer to another question as to how the full-time wardens were appointed, it was stated that this was done solely on merit. Yet another questioner asked whether wardens were really needed at all, given that Hastings was designated a 'safe' area and therefore unlikely to suffer bombing. He implied that the whole thing was a waste of money. Within a year, he was to be proved dreadfully wrong.

In an attempt to lessen the effects of darkness, Summer Time, which was due to end on 8th October, was put back by the government until 19th November. A further change was made on 3rd of November when the black-out was allowed to start half an hour after sunset and to finish half an hour before sunrise. This was later shortened by another 15 minutes. These measures, however, did not prevent two Special Constables from falling off the edge of the unguarded High Street pavement which, in places, rises six feet above road level. One escaped injury, but the other suffered a broken upper arm and was taken to hospital.

November also saw the issuing of respirators for babies. These were quite bulky and required the baby to be placed inside, and for filtered air to be pumped in by hand. Not surprisingly, mothers were filled with apprehension at the prospect of having to put them to serious use whilst pulling on their own respirators, and perhaps those of other young children.

Towards the end of the year, as the hours of black-out lengthened (black-out started at 4.22pm on 23rd December), more casualties occurred. A elderly man was knocked down by a car, near his home in Battle Road, as he went to fetch beer for his supper. He died the next day at the Buchanan Hospital from shock caused by his injuries. Two women were knocked down and injured by cars in the darkness in two other incidents. In another sad occurrence, an elderly man, although he was using a torch, fell on the steps leading from Hughenden Road to Beaconsfield Road where he lived. He suffered a fractured skull, from which he died later in hospital.

By December the local population of some 66,000 had grown by another

100. This figure represented the babies born to expectant evacuee mothers in the maternity ward of St Augustine's Nursing Home.

As 1939 drew to a close, the town prepared for Christmas. This was to be the last one before food rationing began and everyone tried to make the best of things. A number of the evacuees were taken back by their parents to spend Christmas at home and many never returned. Other local families, where the father had been called to military service, found it difficult to find treats, out of a soldier's pay, for their children. Everything considered, efforts were made to keep to the normal arrangements, and the usual Christmas and New Year dances were planned. Local hotels and guest houses were booked to capacity for the festive period, and the Queen's Hotel advertised a Christmas dinner for 12/6 (62$^1/_2$p) which included entertainment and dancing to follow. Children's parties were held in schools for both local and evacuee pupils. At the White Rock Pavilion a great Anglo-French Christmas Circus was staged from 26th to 30th December. An elephant act, performing seals, liberty ponies and a ballerina on horseback, as well as the usual trapeze artists and clowns all put on a marvellous show. The stage had to be extended into the auditorium to accommodate the circus ring, and the orchestra pit moved to one side.

As 1939 drew to a close and the people faced the uncertainties of the year ahead, the words used by King George VI in his Christmas Day broadcast that year, were to be long remembered. *'And I said to the man who stood at the Gate of the Year, 'Give me a light that I may tread safely into the unknown'. And he replied, 'Go out into the darkness, and put your hand into the Hand of God. That shall be to you better than light, and safer than a known way.'*

For the first two weeks of January 1940, Hastings suffered the coldest weather since records began, with 12 inches of snow and 20 degrees of frost. Buses and trains stopped running, and stand pipes sprang up in every street to supply households where the mains inlet had frozen. Strangely enough, although the townspeople were only too well aware of the extreme conditions, they were not allowed to read about them in the local press until two weeks later, because of wartime censorship which imposed a delay on all such reports. Such a desolate start presaged the bleakness of the year that lay ahead.

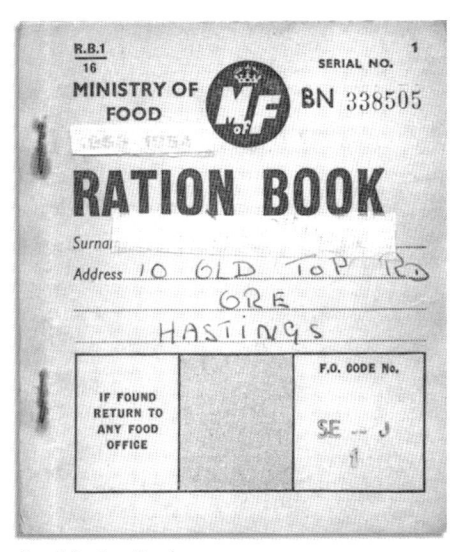

Food Ration Book.

On January 8th, the long-threatened food rationing began. (See appendix II). The first three items per person, per week were: bacon/ham 4oz, butter 2oz, sugar 8oz per person. The tea ration from July 1940 was 2oz.

Black-out accidents continued to occur, but at last in the High Street, and later in Cambridge Road, railings were put up to prevent any more people falling off the edge of the high pavements in the dark.

In March, meat was rationed. Unlike other foods it was rationed by price instead of weight. This meant a choice between a small piece of best steak or a larger quantity of a cheaper cut. Housewives quickly learnt to make the meat ration go as far as possible. The Ministry of Food gave advice on how best to feed the family, and Lord Woolton, the Minister, had the doubtful honour of having the much joked about meatless pie named after him. (See Appendix III)

Innumerable regulations came into force which impinged upon everyone's life. The local court reflected some of these. For instance, a girl was fined for using a bicycle lamp instead of a torch in the black-out. On another occasion a man was fined £2 and had his camera confiscated by the court for taking a photograph of an electricity pylon. He was soundly ticked off by the magistrate and told he was old enough to know better.

The war, phoney or not, did not stop the town making preparations for Easter. All the usual attractions were got ready for the expected influx of visitors. The little boats reappeared on the boating lakes, and the first band concert of the season was given on the pier. Boarding houses and hotels reported excellent bookings. War at that moment seemed remote and, rationing apart, had little impact on our daily lives.

The first prosecution for contravention of the food regulations came when a shop assistant at David Grieg, the grocers, was fined £1 for selling bacon to a customer without asking for coupons. The Company was fined £5.

After Easter, minds were sharply redirected towards the possibility of air attack when the Town Clerk announced that a Casualty Bureau had been set up at the Medical Officer of Health's office in Wellington Square. In the event of death or injury from enemy action all enquiries were to be made there, and on no account were the hospitals or first-aid posts to be asked for news.

10
THE FIGHT BEGINS

On the 10th May 1940, Winston Churchill became Prime Minister when the much-criticised Neville Chamberlain resigned. On the same day, when Hitler began his long-expected and ferocious attack upon his neighbours, our perception of the war changed abruptly. The Luftwaffe bombed the main cities in the Low Countries ahead of the Panzer divisions, which then swept through, crushing all opposition. Such was the might of the German forces, that within nine days, Holland had been vanquished, Belgium had surrendered, and in spite of the good fight put up by the French Armies and the British Expeditionary Force, the Germans were entering France and sweeping across the 1916 battlefields of the Somme. On May 20th, Abbeville and Amiens fell. On the 22nd, the Germans turned northwards towards the ports of Boulogne and Calais which they took on the 25th and 26th. Most of the British and French troops found themselves enclosed in an area around Dunkirk. The speed of events was astonishing. In Hastings, the booming of the guns could be heard as the battle raged on the other side of the channel, and if the enemy was not quite at the door, he was but a short sea trip away. It seemed inevitable that, within days, Hitler's 'Operation Sealion' (see Appendix IV) would be put into action and the enemy would be landing on the British beaches.

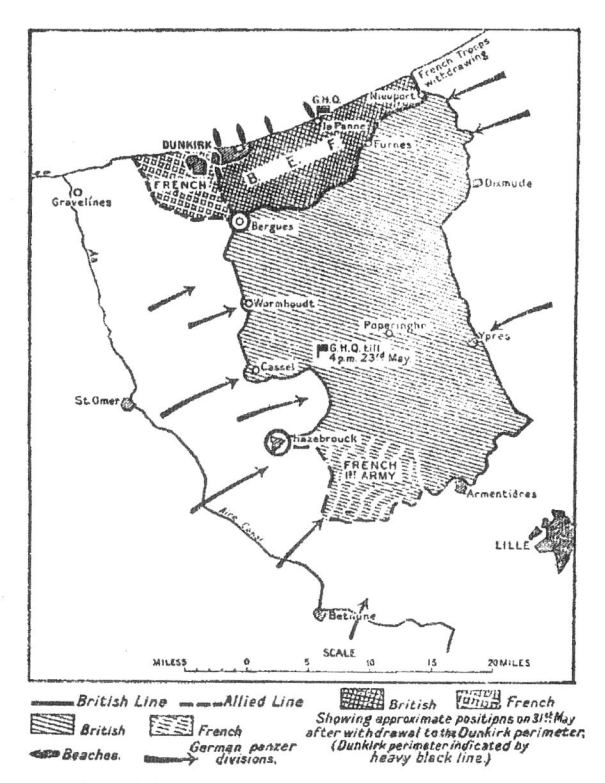

Map of Dunkirk Area prior to evacuation.

It was then that the British naval operation 'Dynamo' began. Vice-Admiral Bertram Ramsay's task was to get as many of our men out of the Dunkirk area as possible. It was estimated that perhaps 30,000 or so could be saved. In the event, over 338,000 British and French troops were rescued. The Admiralty and the Ministry of Shipping sent out calls to owners of all small vessels to report to Dover with their craft as soon as possible. Around 850 vessels of all kinds responded, including 20 RNLI lifeboats from ports all round the coast, from Lowestoft to Poole. Hastings lifeboat, the Cyril and Lilian Bishop, was one of them. Ten of the local fishing boats also set sail for Dover but were not used. The Hastings lifeboat, set off around 4.0 p.m. on 30th May. The Coxwain, George Moon, took Bill Hilder and Will Martin, first and second mechanics, and a scratch crew made up of brothers Bill, Jim and Ted Terrell and three other fishermen. By dusk they had reached Folkestone. At that time, all boats had to be in port before nightfall, or risk being shot at. They put into Folkestone, and spent the night at the Mission to Seamen. Early the next day they continued on to Dover. On arrival, they reported to the naval authorities and were told that they would have to follow a marked course to Dunkirk, to avoid mines. Their request for weapons of some sort, to take with them, was refused, and they were directed to obtain petrol and food for the journey. When the Hastings crew returned to their boat, they were surprised and annoyed to find two sailors on board trying to start the engine. They were informed that the Royal Navy had commandeered the boat and would make the crossing. The Hastings crew were given railway warrants for their return to Hastings, and one can only guess what they were thinking. The lifeboat spent the weekend until 2nd June at Dunkirk and was brought back from Dover by its regular crew on Wednesday, June 5th. When the boat had left Hastings on 30th May it was in pristine condition. On its return, it was in a poor state, leaking, with a hole in the bow, and had obviously been put to heavy use. It also bore signs of having capsized. Fortunately, it was able to be restored with money raised from an appeal.

Among other vessels to respond to operation Dynamo, were paddle steamers belonging to P & A Campbell, which, as mentioned in an earlier

Hastings Lifeboat the 'Cyril and Lilian Bishop' which took part in the Dunkirk evacuation.

chapter, took many carefree holiday-makers on trips from Hastings Pier to France before the war. Sadly, the Brighton Belle and the Brighton Queen were both lost on the beaches of Dunkirk. A Royal Naval Seaman, James Woodhams of Battle, described how he spent the last two days aboard the much-loved Brighton Queen. On the first day, he made seven trips in the ship's lifeboat to shallow water to pick up troops and ferry them to the ship, plugging bullet holes as they went. The Brighton Queen then towed another stranded ship back with them towards Dover. The following day they returned to Dunkirk to pick up French troops from the jetty. On leaving harbour, the ship was bombed and quickly sank. Many men were thrown into the sea but managed to cling to the parts of the ship still projecting above the shallow water. They were picked up after about an hour by a tug, and eventually arrived back in England.

P.S. Brighton Belle

Paddle Steamer, The Brighton Belle.

As the German war machine was smashing its way through Belgium, there was an unexpected happening in Hastings. On 22nd May, a local fisherman, Mr R Mitchell, saw a vessel anchored off the Fairlight cliffs. After hailing it, he went alongside and found it to be a small Belgian steam tug, crowded with French and Belgian refugees. It had dropped anchor with the intention of finding a way ashore. Mr Mitchell piloted it to Hastings Pier. On board were elderly men, women and children, all tired, hungry and soaking wet. Among them were the Financial Director and Chief Engineer of the Belgian Railways. Rather than let the railway's assets fall into German hands, they had left Brussels, some days before, in an attempt to escape to France by road. Travelling in three lorries and one car, they took with them books, records and 13 million Belgian francs, all belonging to the Belgian Railways. They found it impossible to get through. There was chaos and carnage on roads so crowded with refugees, that they had to turn back. Arriving eventually in Antwerp, they abandoned the car and three lorry-loads of documents on the quayside. Under fierce aerial attack they managed to retain two suitcases containing the money, and board the tug on 21st May. They had no charts, compass or radio for the crossing, and had to rely on the tug's mate to navigate his way as best he could. They told of an Antwerp in flames, and numerous boats trying to leave. The Chief Constable, Mr Joseph Bell, took personal charge of the situation, and arranged for all the refugees to be cared for at St Helen's Hospital and for the money to put be into safe-keeping at a bank.

The evacuation of Dunkirk finished on 4th June. Winston Churchill then broadcast to the nation about the threatened German invasion saying, '. . . *we shall defend our island, whatever the cost may be. We shall fight on the beaches, we shall fight on the landing grounds, we shall fight in the fields and in the streets: we shall never surrender.*'

Whilst events were unfolding across the Channel, Hastings was already preparing to defend its own territory. On the 18th May, an appeal was made for local men to join the Local Defence Volunteers (later re-named The Home Guard). Some 800 volunteers, ready to fight for their country, turned up in one day at the local police station to register. These came from all walks of life, from teenagers to retired army officers who had served in the Boer War. It was intended that these men should deal with enemy parachutists, and generally defend the town. Everyone was aware of the danger and was on the watch for signs of the enemy. On one occasion, armed Hastings police rushed to the East Hill following a report that a parachutist had been seen descending in the area. Happily, it turned out to be a partly deflated barrage balloon passing by, some way out to sea.

The police made a sweep of the town on 18th May to round up all enemy aliens. Within 24 hours every German and Austrian living in the Borough had been detained and taken off to be interned for the duration of the war. On the 6th June, all remaining non-enemy aliens were ordered to leave the town and to take themselves at least 20 miles from the coast. Many of them were Italians who had lived and run cafés, ice-cream parlours and restaurants in the town for many years but, on government orders, they all had to go. They were taken in coaches, under police escort, to East Grinstead to make sure they left the area.

A ban was placed on the ringing of church bells, except to signal that an invasion was taking place. Barbed wire barriers appeared in the streets. The seafront railings were festooned with barbed wire from the Old Town to the Bathing Pool at Bo-Peep. Access to the foreshore, one of the great local pleasures, was denied to the public and concrete 'dragons' teeth' were implanted in the beach below the promenade to impede enemy tanks. It was understood that mines were also sown beneath the shingle for the same purpose. Floodlights were installed that could light up and sweep across the beaches. Tank-traps were placed across strategic roads within the town. Ecclesbourne and Fairlight Glens also became minefields. The latter was mined by the Devonshire Regiment and sadly, the officer in charge of the work was killed at the end of the operation as he took a short cut across the area. The map of the minefield, which he was carrying, was also lost in the explosion.

Households were issued with a leaflet headed, 'STAY WHERE YOU ARE'. This told everyone to 'stay put' if the Germans arrived, and that was not advice but a military order. No one was to flee before the enemy, (as the refugees in Belgium and France had done) as that would hamper troops defending the town. All false orders from the enemy were to be ignored. If fighting took place in the neighbourhood, people were to treat it as an air-raid and take cover in a shelter.

On the 21st June a 20-mile wide defence zone was declared, stretching from the Wash to the West Sussex border with Hampshire. No-one was permitted to enter the zone except on business. There were to be no holiday-makers or day-trippers, and residents were told not to invite relatives or friends to visit. All hotels and boarding-houses cancelled their bookings. At the same time, all town and place names, all sign-posts and station names were to be removed from sight or obliterated. (Local trolley buses presented a strange sight by going about marked 'XXXXXXXX Tramways').

The next day, the evacuees from London, who had arrived in September 1939, were re-evacuated to places in Wales and a curfew was imposed along the seafront from 10 p.m. to 5 a.m.

BBC news announcers were instructed to give their names before each bulletin. This simple act prevented enemy broadcasters from infiltrating our information system and listeners quickly got to know the voices of announcers such as John Snagg, Alvar Liddell, Frank Phillips and Stuart Hibberd.

France, Britain's only ally, surrendered to the Germans on 22nd June 1940, leaving Britain completely alone against the might of Hitler's forces. In Hastings, people were only too well aware of that, as they awaited the next development.

11
EVACUATION

On 13th July 1940, in order to safeguard the town against unauthorised persons being in the vicinity of the beach and seafront after dark, it was announced that a curfew would be imposed on the front line to coincide with black-out times.

At the same time, with the threat of a German invasion ever present, the government introduced an evacuation scheme for all school children from the SE coastal zone. Although the scheme was said to be voluntary, Mr W Norman King, the Education Officer, told parents it was their duty 'to support the government' and register their children at their schools. Further pressure was put on the parents by his saying that after the evacuation date, all local schools would close and that any children remaining would have no further opportunity of continuing their education, except at private schools. The evacuation would take place on Sunday, July 21st, when children would be sent to 'agricultural areas' in Bedfordshire and Hertfordshire. In cases where children of one family attended different schools, parents could register all their children at one school to travel together. Only 3,000 Hastings pupils, representing 50% of the school population, of whom the majority were from secondary schools, were evacuated at that time. Many parents chose to keep the family together in times of danger. On evacuation day, a total of 69 coaches arrived at the station at intervals from 7.30 a.m. until 10.30 a.m. The Education Officer, in his assumed role of a latter-day Pied Piper, accompanied the pupils on their journey.

Pre-paid card given to all evacuated children to notify parents of their new address.

A few days later, Mr King reported back to the Education Committee that all was well, the children had settled in, the Grammar School in particular was 'very comfortably settled', and the boys seemed very cheerful. In a letter published in the Hastings Observer on 17th August, one boy did in fact write, *'On behalf of the Hastings evacuees, especially the Hastings Grammar School boys, I would like to tell everyone how happy we are. Our fears when we left Hastings were soon put out of our minds when we found out what jolly sporting people we had come to.'*

He went on to describe the reception town in such detail, that some might have guessed which it was. He concludes, 'Everyday except Sunday, up to August 19th, when we shall start school, we have some sort of sport . . . and on Sundays we go to church, so we have plenty to do to occupy our minds. We are all happy and content, and we shall stay here until the enemy have been defeated, and then we shall come back to good old Hastings'.

The young pupils of Halton School were sent to Berkhampstead, a very rural area in Hertfordshire. They were said, by parents who visited them, to be happy in the village school there and enjoying country life.

However, all was not sweetness and light as one girl remembers, 'My older brother was at the Hastings Grammar School, so I was registered to go with him. I was a pupil at the Hastings High School for Girls, and felt I should have gone with people I knew, but our father decided otherwise. A few days before the evacuation date, we went to the Grammar School in Nelson Road. I, a shy 10-year-old, sat in my brother's classroom for the whole of one morning, among his 16-year-old classmates, all strangers to me, while masters busied themselves with lists and registers. Then we all went home again. On 21st July, we were up very early; mother made us both sandwiches for the journey and we prepared our cases. We reported once more to the school with our belongings and gas-masks. Finally, we all trooped down into Nelson Road and boarded buses for the station. Our parents were told not to come with us'.

'We set off on what seemed to be an interminable journey. The boys kept looking out of the window to see where we were, but because all the station names had been removed they could only guess. I remember the unfamiliar noise of dozens of schoolboys chattering and playing games amongst themselves. I sat there, feeling like an invisible and anonymous speck of humanity, my only hold on reality being the 'dog tag' I wore round my neck bearing my name and identity number. Somehow or other, after a lengthy journey we eventually arrived at St Albans in Hertfordshire at about 4.0 p.m. - not exactly an agricultural area. To this day, the journey remains a mystery tour, because the train did not pass through London. We were taken to a local school, where Girl Guides handed out bottles of school milk and chocolate bars. We then queued up at a table where an official was allocating billets. He gave us a slip of paper with a name and address on it, and told us make our own way there. We set off, but had no idea where to go until someone gave us directions. After we had walked for some time, carrying our luggage, a car drew up beside us and the driver asked where we were going. When we showed him the address, he said we were heading in the wrong direction and offered us a lift. He dropped us outside a semi-detached house. A woman answered our knock, and when we announced ourselves as 'the evacuees', her face fell. "Oh", she said, "but I asked for two boys or two girls, not one of

St Albans Abbey.   (Photo: M S Rodgers)

St Albans School shared by Hastings Grammar School.   (Photo: M S Rodgers)

each". We felt less than welcome. She did, however, ask us in and we were given a cup of tea. She went on to say that she had told the billeting officer that she had no beds or bedding and that he would have to provide them, and that if he did not bring her some, we could not stay. She showed us upstairs to two bedrooms that were completely unfurnished, curtainless and with bare boards. It seemed that she and her husband had not been married for long and had a minimum of things. Later in the evening, a van turned up bringing two canvas camp beds and four blankets, but no pillows. Later that evening we filled in and posted the pre-paid card we had been given to let our parents know our new address. I went to bed, lying on canvas, covered by two scratchy blankets, and shivered all night.

'We stayed in that uncomfortable place for about two months. In the first few weeks before school resumed, I remember going on hikes with the Grammar School scout troop. They were reluctant to include me as they did not think I could keep up the pace. I was determined to prove them wrong. Eventually, my brother resumed lessons with his fellow pupils at St Albans School, which they shared with the local boys. I had nowhere to go, and spent my days wandering around the town, feeling hungry. I spent my small amount of pocket money on bags of broken biscuits from Woolworths. Finally, my brother came home one day and said a master had told him I was to start the next week at St Albans Girls' Grammar School in Fleetville, which I duly did. Again, I knew no-one and was really thrown in at the deep end. Shortly afterwards, my brother heard our landlady complaining to a friend that she really did not want us there. We changed billets with the help of a classmate of my brother's. The new place was better, but the food was poor. I had over two miles to walk to school every day. The premises were shared with Parliament Hill School from London, and we had classes in the mornings only, from 8.30 till 1.0 p.m.'

'I used to leave the house very early, often with no breakfast as the landlady was seldom up. When I got back at about 2.0 p.m. the main meal of the day was over and there was no-one in the house; the landlady having gone out socialising. I had to find whatever was left in the saucepans, and again, I was frequently hungry. The gym mistress eventually noticed that I had lost weight and I was referred to the school clinic. My landlady was asked to accompany me, and was told by the doctor that I was undernourished. The news, which she received with a very bad grace, must have gone quite unheeded because the food, such as it was, never improved. Things went on much the same until the autumn of 1941 when my brother received his exam results and could leave school. We then both returned to Hastings. Our mother was shocked to see how thin we both were.'

Predictably, in the lucky dip of the billeting arrangements, some were very fortunate to find really kind hosts. Bob Wisden, a senior pupil in 1940, found himself in a very welcoming family with whom he kept contact for many years. He remembers the Abbey, the interesting Roman remains at Verulamium, and Gorhambury Park where the scout troop enjoyed camping. Space at school was scarce and he says, 'Exams in my case were written in the garden chalet of the headmaster's house, and invigilated by the his wife. Senior boys were roped in for fire-watching which earned a minimal and very welcome payment'.

It is generally acknowledged by Old Boys of the Hastings Grammar School that their lives were greatly helped by the dedication of the masters who provided continuity and stability. Particular tribute is paid to the scoutmasters, who continued to run the troop and gave the boys valuable training of a practical nature.

Frank Ashworth, who spent four years as an evacuee, had three different hosts - all of them welcoming. In the first home, he only stayed for one term as a change of family circumstances necessitated a move. He then went to a well-connected family. He says, '. . . I had to enlarge my social skills to breakfast from the sideboard, the proper address to a knight of the realm and his wife (parents of my host) and to the cook, and occasional encounters with such dinner guests as the Dean - complete with apron and gaiters. I was with them for two years and they treated me very much as one of the family.' He spent the last year and a half of his time at St Albans with an elderly couple, of whom the husband was a sidesman at the Abbey. He kept in touch until 1960 when the wife, by then a widow, died and he was able to read the lesson at her funeral in the Abbey.

Another Hastings girl, Brenda Glazier said, 'I was evacuated to St Albans with my cousin who was at Ore Girls' School. We had been there only about a week when her mother came to visit. She took my cousin back with her the same day, leaving me on my own, and I was very upset. I was desperately unhappy there and then one day, some weeks later, I was walking in St Peter's

Street (the main street of the town) *when, to my surprise, I saw my father walking towards me. I flung myself into his arms and begged him to take me home. He had come to St Albans on a job for Bryant's, the Hastings removal firm that he worked for, and it was by pure chance that we met. In spite of all my pleading, he refused absolutely to take me back. He gave no reason except to say he couldn't. I was left distraught'.*

Much later, she learnt that the reason for her father's refusal was that his nephew, Clifford Glazier, aged 14, had just been killed by a bomb on Monday, September 30th, outside the Plaza Cinema in Hastings. For obvious reasons, he could not tell his young daughter, who was heartbroken and quite unable to understand why he appeared to reject her. Eventually, Brenda was allowed to return to Hastings after about 8 months away, when her parents had had time to reconsider things.

Around 155 pupils from Hastings High School for Girls were evacuated to Ware in Hertfordshire where they shared the Girls' Grammar School.

Just five days after the evacuation trains left Hastings, the first air-raid took place, killing a woman teacher. Priory Road Schools, which were by then closed down, were badly damaged. One could say the children were well out of it.

That attack was followed by four more in August. These gave rise to a second voluntary evacuation, in early September, which was open to all remaining children, including those under school age, and mothers who wished to leave. Mothers of children evacuated in the first wave were told they could choose to join them, although this was a hope rather than a reality. One mother, after lining up with hundreds of others at the station, was told that the last available seat on the train to her chosen town had just been taken. She rushed off to find her husband at his place of work, to ask what she should do, and was told, 'Go, wherever they send you'. She was put on another train for an unknown destination and after an all-night journey, found herself in Bridgewater in Somerset. Her husband stayed behind as a key worker in Hastings, and thus

Priory Road School bombed on 26th July 1940 with inset of damaged classroom.

the family was scattered in three different counties. The mother was given a billeting allowance of 5/- per week (25p) which paid for a room only. There were many such cases where the husband's resources were stretched to the limit. He had to continue to pay the overheads of the family home in Hastings, maintain himself, and support his evacuated wife. In addition, from August, the local Council asked parents to contribute 6/- per week (30p) towards the billeting costs of each evacuated child. In some cases the rates went unpaid, and the Council had to make special arrangements for deferment.

BLACK-OUT TIMES

Week commencing August 17th.

	Begins	Ends
Saturday	8.48 p.m.	5.18 a.m.
Sunday	8.47 p.m.	5.19 a.m.
Monday	8.45 p.m.	5.21 a.m.
Tuesday	8.43 p.m.	5.22 a.m.
Wednesday	8.41 p.m.	5.24 a.m.
Thursday	8.39 p.m.	5.26 a.m.
Friday	8.37 p.m.	5.27 a.m.

The curfew in the Front Line area begins at 10 p.m. and lasts till 5 a.m.

Blackout and Curfew times, August 1940.

12
THE BOMBING STARTS

From the first air-raid on 26th July 1940, until the end of the war in 1945, Hastings suffered 85 visits from Hitler's Luftwaffe. In all, 154 lives were lost, 260 people received serious injuries, and 439 had lesser injuries. From the first conventional bomb in July 1940, to the last flying bomb on 28th August 1944, a total of 550 H.E. bombs and 15 flying bombs fell on the town (see map). In addition there were 12 oil incendiary bombs and 750 small incendiary bombs. A considerable number of other bombs fell in the sea and caused no damage or casualties. In the town there was widespread damage to property. A total of 463 houses were demolished or beyond saving, and 14,818 other properties were damaged.

These figured are just that - figures. They give no clear picture of the tragedy and suffering which the townspeople endured, nor do they reflect the courage and determination of those called upon to cope with the events as they happened. There seemed no obvious reason for these attacks save that of trying to terrorise and soften the country up for Hitler's planned invasion. The killing and maiming of civilians in a peaceful seaside town could hardly be classed as a military objective.

The London Blitz began in September 1940 and continued until May 1941. In Hastings, during that period, Hitler's bombers could be heard droning overhead on their way to and from the capital. At the same time, on a smaller scale, Hastings experienced a period of intense aerial attacks. At one time, the sound of air-raid warnings was a constant feature of daily life.

The first raid on the town came early one morning.

Friday, July 26th.

Mr Bob Tester, a serving police officer at the time recalls, *'It happened about 7.15 in the morning. It was just one plane. I looked out of the window of the Town Hall and saw bombs landing in the Cricket Ground. They didn't do any damage - just threw up the earth. Up on the West Hill, other bombs had fallen in Priory Road and around the top of Whitefriars Road. A woman teacher, a Mrs Gooday, was killed. She was the first person to be killed in Hastings. A lot of others were injured. The bombs were quite small - 50 pounders.'*

The plane responsible, on that occasion, was a lone bomber which dropped 11 bombs in all. In addition to Mrs Gooday, who died in a house in Priory Road, there were nine other people injured, two of them seriously.

Wednesday, August 14th.

A single bomber dropped six H.E.s in the Bexleigh Avenue area. Two people were killed.

HASTINGS IN THE SECOND WORLD WAR (1939–45)   SITES OF H.E. BOMBS

Map showing all H.E. bombs, including V1s, which fell on Hastings.

Thursday, August 15th.

A number of bombers broke away from a formation of 50 - 60 planes flying up the channel. Bombs fell in the St Leonards area, some on the beach and others out to sea, leaving one dead and two injured.

Wednesday, August 21st.

A single bomber dropped two H.E.s causing widespread damage but slight casualties.

Friday, August 23rd.

One H.E bomb and one oil bomb were dropped on open ground at Ecclesbourne Glen and Barley Lane.

The Battle of Britain which began on 10th July 1940 was fought mainly over Kent, but some of its effects spread to Hastings. On August 25th, a German bomber, riddled by bullets from a Spitfire, crashed in flames a mile offshore. Four of the crew of five perished with the plane, but the 25-year-old pilot baled out, Hastings lifeboat was launched, and he was rescued an hour later about a mile from where the plane came down. By chance, the engine of the lifeboat had cut out, and the pilot's cries for help could be heard. As he was hauled aboard, shivering in his life jacket, he received a mixed reception. He was first given a pullover by one of the crew, and then a hefty kick. On being brought ashore in front of a hostile crowd, he gave a Nazi salute which brought forth a cry of *'Hit the b......... with an oar'*. However, wiser counsel prevailed, and he was handed over to the military in case he was of use to the intelligence services.

The second voluntary evacuation, mentioned in the previous chapter, took place on Wednesday, 11th September. This time, because bombing had started, it was more of a mass exodus. 14,000 left by special trains, and 5000 by special railway coaches. Many thousands more preferred to make their own arrangements. Rather than take pot luck in a strange billet in a strange town, they preferred to go to relatives or friends. The population more than halved overnight, from the pre-war figure of around 65,000 to 34,000.

Another incident in the Battle of Britain occurred on 15th September. An air battle, which started over London between a squadron of Hurricanes and German bombers, ended over the cliffs at Fairlight. One bomber crashed just outside the town and the crew of three were captured. Two other bombers disappeared out to sea chased by fighters, which later returned giving the 'victory roll'. One British fighter pilot baled out of his burning plane and landed in a tree, where he hung for some time before being rescued.

On 24th September, a large German bomber was chased out to sea by two fighters. Smoke was seen to come from the plane as it lost height and fell into the sea.

On the outskirts of the town on 25th September, a Messerschmitt fighter-bomber crashed at Beaney's lane on the Ridge. The crew of two perished. One baled out too low and was killed, the other died in the crash.

September and October brought with them many more air attacks on the town. The casualty lists were lower than they might have been because so many houses were uninhabited - their occupiers having left in the preceding evacuation. Nevertheless, precious lives were lost, homes reduced to rubble and a lot of business property destroyed. The air-raid sirens seemed to wail all the time, and those left in the town spent much of their time dashing for shelter. All was made much worse by the fact that Hastings had no anti-aircraft guns until 14th October, and was therefore at the mercy of the German planes. The only defence was the occasional appearance of RAF fighters which, in the main, were heavily engaged elsewhere. Consequently, the bombers were free to come in, sometimes more than once in the day, circle the town as they pleased, drop their bombs and then make off back across the channel. In September there were 16 attacks.

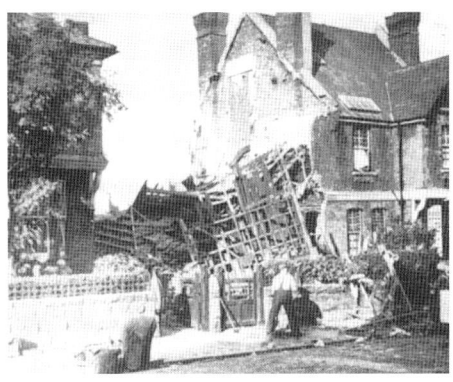

Bomb damage in St Peter's Road, 10th September 1940.

Monday, September 9th.

A German plane, chased by a British fighter during an air battle, dropped several bombs in the sea.

Tuesday, September 10th.

Nine H.E. bombs were dropped in Hollington Park, The Green, and Tower Road area of St Leonards, leaving two dead and other casualties. A number of incendiaries were also dropped.

Thursday, September 12th.

15 H.E.s and 150 incendiaries were dropped in the Clive Vale area, killing two people and injuring others.

Saturday, Sepember 14th.

H.E.s fell in Linton Crescent in an attempt to bomb the railway. The Old town had a lucky escape when a stick of nine bombs fell in a line up All Saints street to High Wickam but failed to explode.

Friday, September 20th.

H.E.s fell near Ore railway tunnel and at Batchelor's Bump causing a fire.

Sunday, September 22nd.

Four H.E.s exploded around Mount Pleasant Church after lunch, causing damage to the church. Eleven others fell among strollers in Alexandra Park, but failed to explode.

Monday, September 23rd.

In the densely populated area of Halton, 60 people were made homeless, a husband and wife were killed, and many injured when three HEs and an oil bomb were dropped.

Halton Schools destroyed on 23rd September 1940.

Tuesday, September 24th.

There were two separate raids in which a total of 33 H.E.s and one oil bomb fell. Three people were seriously injured, and another slightly.

Wednesday, September 25th.

There were two more raids in one day on Central St Leonards, where a total of 18 H.E.s fell. Three people were killed and 16 seriously injured.

Thursday, September 26th.

There were two separate raids during the afternoon when 40 H.E.s were dropped. The gasholders and the railway station were attacked as well as houses in Queens Road and the vicinity, where three people were killed. Properties were also destroyed in Clive Vale and central St Leonards causing a number of casualties.

Saturday, September 28th.

The Bexhill Road and Seaside Road district came under attack when 14 H.E.s fell.

Sunday, September 29th.

The Croft Road and Salter's Lane area of the Old Town were badly damaged when 18 H.E.s fell.

Monday, September 30th.

Bombs fell in Bexhill Road. In the Town Centre, one hit the Plaza Cinema, (now Yates' Wine Bar) on the opposite side of the road to Debenham's. Eight people were killed outright, others, horribly mutilated, died later, bringing the death toll to 14. 12 more were seriously hurt and 23 slightly injured.

This last incident is remembered in the town as one of the most tragic incidents of 1940. It happened at 10.30 in the morning while an air battle was taking place overhead and many people were, out in the street, watching it. The H.E. bomb, which hit the coping high up on the cinema, exploded in mid air. The dead included the first young person to be killed in the Borough. He was 14-year-old Clifford Glazier, an office employee, who had been out to post a letter. The cinema manager was also killed, as well as the secretary of the Hastings Pier Company, together with QMS Southey of the Hastings Home Guard and his wife. All four faces of the Memorial clock tower were blown out. October brought no respite, when there were 20 raids.

Plaza Cinema. The damage to the coping above the letters PL shows where the bomb struck before exploding in mid-air.

Wednesday, October 2nd.

One bomb, which exploded in White Rock gardens, threw debris crashing through the roof of the children's ward of the Royal East Sussex Hospital across the road. Luckily the ward was not in use. In all 16 bombs were dropped.

Friday, October 4th.

16 H.E.s and two oil bombs were dropped in two separate raids. St Leonards Pier was damaged. One person was killed and four seriously injured.

Saturday, October 5th.

There were four attacks in one day. Between 8 a.m. and 9 a.m. three attacks occurred in which 17 bombs fell but caused no casualties. A worse attack came

Ruins of the Bedford Public House in Queens Road which suffered a direct hit on October 5th 1940.

Abbey National Offices now stand on the same site.

at 11.29 a.m. when 12 bombs were dropped, one of which scored a direct hit on the Bedford pub on the corner in Queen's Road where the Abbey National Office now stands. Others fell in the Cricket Ground, Wallinger's Walk and the Old Town. In all, eight people were killed, eight seriously injured, and others less badly hurt. One victim of the Bedford bombing was the unfortunate street trader who kept a barrow in the street at the side. He was buried under the debris and died. Others buried in the ruins included the landlord and his wife who were safely extricated, but two others died. Invaluable assistance was rendered on that occasion by the trained ARP staff from nearby Marks and Spencer who were on the spot immediately. In that same raid, a man and woman escaped uninjured from the van in which they were travelling when it was blown upside down by a bomb exploding in the road behind them.

Monday, October 7th.

A man was trapped from 6 p.m. until midnight in the ruins of his house in Stockleigh Road after a single high blast bomb fell. Rescue parties worked on tirelessly, in great danger, as darkness fell. The victim was trapped by his injured foot and bearing a great weight on his body. By careful shoring up, or cutting away in places, the rescue teams finally succeeded in releasing him. Six other people were seriously hurt and four injured.

Tuesday, October 8th.

Bombs fell in the Town Centre, when Havelock Road, York Buildings and the sea front opposite Pelham Arcade were bombed. Two oil bombs were also dropped. One of the three dead, a young woman, was not found until some days later in an office in Havelock Road. Ten other people were injured. One enemy plane flew for a long time over the town that day, taking several runs over the railway station before releasing the heaviest bomb up to that time. This was a 2,000-pounder which fell harmlessly on allotments behind Braybrooke Road.

Wednesday, October 9th.

Over 20 H.E.s were dropped in three different raids. Three people were killed, three seriously injured and eight others hurt. The incidents were mainly in the Old Town and Ore districts.

Thursday, October 10th.

25 H.E.s were dropped in two raids, killing one person and injuring two more.

Saturday, October 12th.

Two H.E.s fell in the morning near the station. The fighter-bombers returned in the afternoon to the same area, in a more determined attack. Using dive bombing tactics they dropped 11 H.E.s and two oil bombs. Gasholders, which used to stand on the site now occupied by Safeways, were holed and set alight. Mr Reginald Gant a 26-year-old employee of Southern Railway and member of the Southern Railway Home Guard, went to the scene to have a look. He helped the AFS to get their hoses in position, then climbed to the top of one gasholder from which flames were pouring. He helped others plug the hole with clay. Then, unaided, he tackled another hole in the side of the holder where fierce flames, forced out by the pressure within, threatened an adjacent holder. He was in great danger of being burned and had to rely on the accuracy of the fire-fighters as they played their hoses to cool the area. As it was, he *'got well singed'*. He worked alone for about half an hour until he succeeded in plugging the hole. For his brave and selfless deed, which averted a major disaster, he was awarded the George Medal.

Sunday, October 13th.

Two H.E. bombs fell at Kite's Farm, Harley Shute Road.

On Monday October 14th, which happened to be the anniversary of the Battle of Hastings, the first anti-aircraft guns appeared in the town.

Thursday, October 17th.

Two H.E. bombs fell at Tilekiln Lane, Fairlight Road.

Saturday, October 26th.

Another attack was made on Halton when a salvo of bombs fell on unoccupied houses and a small Mission Hall in Priory Road. There were four casualties, two of them serious.

Tuesday, October 29th.

While an air battle was in progress, two bombs fell at the top of Linton Road. They were dropped from a great height by a Dornier. Two people were hurt.

November brought a slight easing in the frequency of the attacks:

Sunday, November 10th.

20 H.E.s fell in three raids during the morning in Fairlight Road, Bexhill Road and Harley Shute, and Buckshole reservoir in Alexandra Park. One person was killed and two seriously injured.

Monday, November 11th.

18 H.E.s fell on that Armistice Day. Broomgrove Power Station was the target, but it was not hit. Mercatoria and Maze Hill were also affected.

Tuesday, November 26th.

West Marina Station in Bexhill Road was the target, and houses in the vicinity were damaged. Three people were injured, one seriously. This raid took place as an air battle was in progress during which two German planes were shot down into the sea. The year closed without further bombing.

Even during those dangerous times, everyday life in Hastings continued on another level.

In October, a body wearing an Iron Cross was found drowned on the shore at Ecclesbourne Glen. It was that of Friedrich Ziel, a German airman aged about 36.

The court continued to see its monotonous parade of black-out offenders, those who did not observe the nightly curfew, and others who ignored the ban on entering the town from outside the defence zone.

The first prosecution for breach of the curfew was on 3rd September. A local woman was found, drunk, in a shelter by the Old Town boating lake at 10.40 p.m. She had no permit to be out late, and when told to move on, she became abusive and hysterical. She was charged under the Defence Regulations for breach of curfew and fined £1. She was fined a further £1 for being drunk and disorderly.

In October, the Council conjured up pastoral scenes in the war-torn town by deciding to allow sheep to graze on public recreation grounds such as the East and West Hills, the Pilot Field and St Leonards golf course.

At the height of the London blitz, two pumps from Hastings Fire Service were sent to London at very short notice, to help the London brigade. Their crews towed the pumps to London and all were put to immediate use all through the night. The men returned to Hastings the next day but left the pumps behind for further use. Further help was given when several groups of 20 London Firemen were brought to Hastings for much-needed seven-day breaks. An equal number of local men replaced them in London.

The Defence Area regulations were strictly enforced, as was evident In December when police were called to an hotel in Warrior Square to interview a man who had just arrived. He said he had travelled to Hastings from London Bridge. He had bought his ticket despite large notices at London stations telling people they must not go to certain areas. He could not satisfy police that he had a special reason for coming, and was eventually sent to prison for one month.

When the bombing started in 1940, whole families, mainly from the Old Town, took refuge in St Clement's Caves which formed a huge, natural, air-raid shelter. (These are now open to the public as The Smuggler's Adventure). Five hundred bunk beds and new toilets were installed, as well as facilities for cooking. A new doorway was knocked through into Croft Road, giving easy access for the Old Towners. Those who chose to take up such a subterranean existence seemed quite content to go on living there for as long as necessary. They ate together, organised their sleeping and catering arrangements, and generally adapted themselves to living as a community underground. One, possibly apocryphal, story is that one of the Old Town fisherman was sent to buy meat for the whole community of several hundred people. At the butcher's he said, 'I want 'arf a sheep!'

By the time the festive season approached, the Memorial clock, which had been badly damaged in September, began to tell the time again.

At Christmas, Sir Auckland Geddes, the Commissioner for Civil Defence for the South East, sent a message to all in his region. He said that there had been 4,000 air attacks throughout the area, and that tens of thousands of bombs had fallen on Kent and Sussex homes. He then thanked all police, fire-fighters, wardens, casualty services, rescue squads, repair parties and WVS for a job well done.

On that note, 1940, the year in which the townspeople had undergone so much separation, suffering, loss of life and damage, finally came to an end.

13
THE SHADOW OF INVASION

Early in 1941, the Medical Officer of Health made a professional visit to St Clement's Caves and reported that *'there was a distinct improvement in the children's condition and there was an air of well-being and happiness about them. Their welfare officers were doing excellent work, and children were receiving instruction and being exercised in the open air'.*

On an official inspection later in the year the Civil Defence Commissioner for the S.E. was impressed by the arrangements, which included a fully equipped welfare clinic, sick bay, and dining hall. He remarked that it was, in his view, the best air-raid shelter in the country.

At the same time, it was found that numerous other children, evacuated the previous year, had been brought back to Hastings by their parents. No doubt this was partly because the children had come home for Christmas and not gone back, and partly because of the levy placed, in August 1940, upon the parents for each evacuated child. The Education Officer was highly critical of the parents' actions and said that he could provide no schooling for their children. No school could be reopened until there was a safe air-raid shelter provided, and this was not yet the case. However, there were plans to remedy this and to re-open three schools when possible. In addition to the 'returnees' there were also many other children, still in the town, who had never left.

The German invasion, thought to be imminent the previous summer, seemed to have been delayed while the bombing of London was being carried out. In Hastings, the Luftwaffe sought to remind us of its presence by continuing to bomb the town.

The Fire Service renewed its advice on how to deal with incendiary bombs. Unlike present-day thoughts on security, we were told to make sure that our houses were easy to enter. We were to have water, sand and a long rake handy, know where there was a ladder, and clear our attics of flammable materials. We were urged to deal with such bombs quickly, as their purpose was to light up an area so that following planes could direct their H.E. bombs.

The Luftwaffe visits to the town began to include night raids.

Saturday, 11th January

A small attack took place at 8.45 p.m. when a number of incendiary bombs were dropped, causing fires in the vicinity of St Margaret's Road.

Sunday, 12th January

A lone bomber circled the town unleashing bursts of machine-gun fire and damaging roofs.

Friday, 31st January

A lone raider, chased by a fighter, dropped 5 H.E.s. A house in Clyde Road was demolished and damage caused in Gensing Road and Woodland Vale Road. Two bombs failed to explode. One person was seriously injured.

In February, obligatory firewatching was introduced. All men aged 16 to 60 were liable to serve up to 48 hours per month. Both private and business premises were included, and in some cases firewatchers received a subsistence allowance of 3/- per night. This was welcome pocket money to some young sixteen-year-olds.

In the drive to 'Grow More Food', idle acres were to be ploughed within the borough. The appropriately named Mr Cherry of the Parks and Gardens department was put in charge of the work. The Harrow Lane football pitch, land belonging to the Grammar School governors at Pine Avenue, council land at Red Lake, and the lower field at Summerfields were all included. Tomatoes would be grown in Alexandra Park, and beetroots in the seafront beds.

With so many children without schools to go to, it was inevitable that some of them would get into trouble. In February, at the Juvenile Court, nine young boys appeared for various offences. The chairman remarked that, *'It is a lamentable state of affairs, and the Education Committee should make some provision for such children. They are running wild, and Satan has found mischief, of the worst sort, for idle hands to do'*. All the boys had been brought back from reception areas. Two brothers, aged 13 and 10, were said to have stolen money from a PDSA box. Their mother told the court she had brought her sons back because they had been turned out of three billets. One of them was already on probation from the court at Hatfield.

At the March meeting of the Education Committee, it was stated that there were some 2,000 children of school age in the town. They were said to be *'on the streets and out of hand'*. A harsh proposal, to clear them from the town by compulsory evacuation, was defeated. Instead, parents were urged not to bring any more children home in the approaching Easter Holidays.

In the same month, Hastings Council was in serious financial trouble because of a sharp fall in income. Hotels and other highly-rated premises had closed down, many houses were standing empty, half the business population had gone, and trade in the town was in severe depression. A reported deficit of £200,000 meant the Council was unable to balance its budget. It was resolved that the Council should apply to the Government for financial assistance.

Rationing of food, although not welcomed, was accepted as a necessary and fair system, provided everyone kept to the rules. The whole subject was treated very seriously, and anyone caught cheating was frowned upon by the general public, and severely dealt with by the courts. Food retailers had to send in forms to the Food Office in Wellington Place to account for everything bought and sold. Sometimes, in poor areas, customers could not afford to buy their full entitlement, which left an opening for the unscrupulous. On one occasion, a couple, who kept a shop, were accused of 'disposing of nearly two hundredweight of rationed goods in excess of what they were entitled to'. Six summonses relating to butter, sugar and margarine were dealt with by the court. The Chairman of the Bench said that the offences were very serious, and liable to incur a heavy fine or imprisonment. Fines of £2, plus costs, were imposed for each of the six offences. (At that time the average man's wage was £4 per week).

We also learnt in March, that a Spitfire, paid for by £5,000 raised in the town the previous August, had been named after the town. The air attacks were resumed the following month

Royal East Sussex Hospital, Cambridge Road, damaged by a direct hit during a night raid on 8th April 1941.

St Helen's Hospital Laundry, destroyed by a direct hit on 8th April 1941.

Tuesday, 8th April.

A sharp night raid took place in which 28 H.E.s and 300 incendiary bombs were dropped. Two hospitals both received direct hits and two nurses were injured. The Municipal Hospital laundry was wrecked. At the Royal East Sussex Hospital, a young nurse, Miss Dorothy Gardner, showed great courage in saving a patient's life during the attack. Hearing a bomb falling, she flung herself across a patient's bed as masonry fell on them. She suffered severe head injuries herself, which kept her in hospital for many long months. The George Medal she was awarded for her brave action is kept in Hastings Museum.

Thursday, 17th April.

At 4.10 a.m. a single bomb fell in the road in Elphinstone Avenue, damaging nearby houses. One resident was seriously hurt and others slightly injured.

Saturday, 26th April.

Two H.E.s fell.

Monday, 16th June.

200 incendiaries were dropped, in the early hours, around the Broomgrove Power Station. In the firewatchers' hut, Mr G C Taylor was asleep when one of the bombs came through the roof and landed on his shoulder. He received severe burns and was later taken to hospital in a serious condition. His colleague, Mr Frank Eastes, who had gone to his assistance was himself severely burned on the hands. For his action he was awarded the BEM.

War Weapons Week, which had been held from 10th to 17th May, more than met its target of £200,000. The money raised was loaned to the Government in the form of War Savings. An indicator panel, showing the amount of money being raised, was erected against the Memorial clock tower. This was designed and executed by students at the Hastings School of Art. Surprisingly, a total of £370,940 was raised from a much reduced population.

Following the sinking of HMS Hood on 25th May, four Hastings families had been notified of the loss of their men. These were, PO H Winfield, Marine R S Miles, A/PO Jack Moon, and PO H E Richer.

Clothes rationing was announced on a Whit Sunday, June 1st, to take effect immediately. This prevented any panic buying. Everyone was given 66 coupons for that year, and some of these had to be given up each time an item of clothing was bought (see Appendix V). In later years the number of coupons was reduced. Hats were not rationed as these were regarded as morale boosters. Rationing meant that all garments had to last as long as possible. Booklets entitled 'Make do and Mend' showed how to lengthen dresses for growing children, how to remake frayed trouser turn-ups, and how to re-use the best parts of worn out garments. Socks were darned, elbows patched, old knitted jumpers were unravelled and the wool re-used. In short, nothing was thrown away or wasted.

Indicator panel erected for War Weapons Week in May 1941 showing money raised.

HMS HOOD

HMS Hood, the Battle Cruiser in which Hastings men were lost when it was sunk by the Bismark on 24th May 1941.

Identity Cards, which everyone was obliged to carry at all times, were generally accepted as a necessary wartime measure. However, not everyone conformed to the rules. One lady from Bexhill, stopped by a police officer in St Leonards, failed to produce her card. When told to produce it at the Bexhill Police Station within two days, she replied, *'I shall do nothing of the sort'*. She failed to comply, and was later fined 20/- (£1).

Looting from bombed or unoccupied houses was viewed especially seriously. In the worst circumstances it carried the death penalty, or penal servitude for life. A Hastings man, who had engaged in widespread looting from bomb-damaged property, received four prison sentences with hard labour: two of twelve months and two of six months, to run concurrently.

The government arranged for the laying in of emergency stores of food in every town and village. In Hastings, stores of corned beef, tinned soup, sugar, condensed milk, margarine and tea were locked away in the underground car-parks. In addition, a record of all private wells in the area was drawn up by the police so that a water supply might be maintained.

In June, three small areas of the beach were

Make Do and Mend booklet.

re-opened for sea bathing from 7.30 a.m. until sunset. An unfortunate result was that a father and his 17-year-old daughter were both drowned at West St Leonards shortly afterwards. A police officer, called to the scene, said that in other circumstances the 'no bathing' flags would have been flying.

The Blitz on London and other major cities was intended to crush the nation's spirit. It was believed that when it ended, Hitler would carry out his plans to invade. In March 1941 we, in the South East, received a leaflet entitled, 'WHAT YOU SHOULD KNOW ABOUT INVASION DANGER'. In it, we were told that everyone who had somewhere to go, outside the defence area, and could be spared, should leave immediately. This applied particularly to school children, mothers with young children, the aged and infirm, pensioners, and the unemployed. As an inducement, railway fares and billeting allowances would be paid. A list of essential workers who were to stay behind was given. These included, police, fire-fighters, lifeboat crews, ARP workers, medical personnel and chemists, council employees, ministers of religion, transport workers, electricity, gas and water workers, and bank employees. The leaflet went on to say, *'When invasion is upon us, evacuation of the remaining population would then be compulsory and at short notice, in crowded trains, with scant luggage, to destinations chosen by the Government. It you are not among the essential workers, go now while the going is good'.*

Compulsory Evacuation Plans

It is not known how many Hastings people responded to this advice, but in June, fresh leaflets and posters were distributed in the town. These ordered compulsory registration of all children, aged between five and fourteen, during the week ending 28th June. We were warned that it was an offence, incurring a fine or imprisonment under the Defence Regulations, not to comply. At the same time, the local police were given the job of devising secret plans for the compulsory evacuation of the town.

A detailed and wide ranging scheme, covering all 'non-essential' people still in the town, was drawn up. It was estimated that these numbered some 34,000 people including 7,200 children. The children would be sent away first, followed by the adult population. About 4,000 key people would be kept back to defend the town and keep essential services running. The plan would remain secret, and no posters or other advance information published, for fear of causing alarm. When the moment came for action, the Borough Police (of whom there were, at that time, 116 regular officers with 14 vacancies, 50 auxiliaries and 200 special constables), would inform every household at very short notice, by knocking on doors and instructing them individually to go, on foot, to one of four railway stations at a given hour. Hand bills would be left for those not at home. In the worst case, the walk to the station could have been anything up to three miles, and at night. The routes were to be by the back streets, to leave the main roads clear. It was reckoned that 44 trains would be required, and these would leave at half-hourly intervals. Only one item of luggage was to be carried per person. The evacuees would be sent to various towns to the south of London, from Reigate in Surrey as far as Bromley and Orpington in Kent. Anyone who could not possibly travel, i.e. the blind or invalids, would stay behind and be accommodated in various nursing homes in the town. All domestic animals would be put down. Elaborate arrangements were worked out as to how a second case of belongings could be labelled, placed in depots in the town, and be forwarded later to the owners. To that end, a list of every commercial vehicle registered in the town was drawn up, ranging from removal lorries to grocery vans.

The 4,000 'essential' people remaining would live in rest centres, and be fed communally at existing catering establishments, such as Woolworths, the Ritz cinema or others which had spacious enough facilities for such a service. Woolworths, for one, willingly agreed to provide 1000 meals three times per day, provided they could have sufficient food supplies and extra tableware to do so.

What you should know about
INVASION DANGER

You will shortly receive a leaflet "Beating the Invader," issued to all householders in the country, telling you what to do should invasion come. If invasion finds you in this town, and you are not ordered to leave, you must act on the instructions to stand firm. But you can help to defeat the invader by leaving now if you can be spared and have somewhere to go.

THIS APPLIES PARTICULARLY TO—
SCHOOL CHILDREN
MOTHERS WITH YOUNG CHILDREN
AGED AND INFIRM PERSONS
PERSONS LIVING ON PENSIONS
PERSONS WITHOUT OCCUPATION OR LIVING IN RETIREMENT

Advice on leaving the coastal area, issued in March 1941.

Fortunately, this scheme was never to be put into action, although those in charge of defending our shores evidently still thought an invasion would come, as a well-guarded secret method of repelling the invader was devised. This was a twentieth century equivalent of 'pouring boiling oil from the ramparts'. Huge circular metal tanks, encased in brickwork, appeared in the town. Two were high up in White Rock Gardens, another by the Old Town boating lake, and yet another at Rock-a-Nore. These were filled with oil, and were not unlike Martello Towers in appearance, They were linked to one another by a pipeline, also protected by brickwork, which ran down to the beach and along to Rock-a-Nore. When the enemy landed, the oil would be released and ignited, by chemical means, when it came into contact with water, thus setting the landing beaches on fire and ensuring a warm welcome to the visitors. We were never to find out how well it might have worked as, in June 1941, Hitler turned his attention elsewhere, with his invasion of Russia.

It was already an offence to leave a vehicle at night without immobilising it. From August, an additional order was made that all unlicensed vehicles and motorcycles were to be immobilised. Distributor heads or sparking plugs had to be removed, packaged, and labelled with the owner's name and address, and handed in to the nearest Police Station.

In August, a local man of 24 was sent to prison for six months for refusing to obey a court order to undergo a medical examination for military service. He had registered as a conscientious objector as he *'was not prepared to participate in the present madness'*. The tribunal had taken his name off the register. His appeal was refused, and he was ordered to report for a medical, which he twice failed to attend.

In the same month another war-victim was washed up at Bo-Peep minus arms, head and feet. He was clothed in an airman's uniform, and papers revealed him to be Wiadyslaw Zolnewski, a Polish airman. His remains were recovered by the police and taken away, by the RAF, for burial.

Members of the Womens' Land Army were at work in Alexandra Park as part of the drive to 'Grow more Food' The harvest that year brought a bumper crop of onions from the former flower beds. In the countryside, large numbers of local people could be seen picking blackberries, for which they were paid 3d per pound. The fruit was to be bottled or made into jam, and used at local feeding centres.

The Ministry of Home Security announced that from 8th November, the ban on people entering the defence area was to be partially lifted until 5th February 1942. The coast from Hastings to Littlehampton was once more open to visitors. However, we were warned that the concession might be cancelled at any moment. Outsiders were still forbidden to take up permanent residence, and no-one was to travel into the area without good reason. The news was generally welcomed as it meant that the feeling of isolation felt by coastal dwellers was dispelled. In December of that year, in the hope that the threat of invasion had gone away, we all looked forward to being able to spend Christmas with family members.

14
HIT AND RUN

Thursday, 1st January.

The first day of 1942 brought a change in German tactics. They started to use machine guns and/or cannons, as well as dropping bombs. In one incident, a train was attacked on its way to Hastings. When it arrived in the station it was seen to be riddled with bullet holes. The guard, who was injured in the incident, was taken to hospital. In the same attack, a bus had its tyres ripped to shreds.

Monday, 5th January

Two raiders opened fire with machine guns. A woman was hit in the leg which later had to be amputated.

Sunday, 1st February.

A German plane machine-gunned a defenceless Hastings fishing boat, whilst it was at sea. Mr James Phillips, aged 69, one of the three men on board, died in the boat.

Salvage became a vital activity. Metal gates and railings were removed from Alexandra Park, the Cricket Ground, Horntye Allotments and from various churches around the town. A total of 300 tons was gathered up in the first month of the year, and transported by rail to be used for weapons. Waste paper also became a precious commodity. From March, it was an offence to burn or destroy paper and cardboard or to dispose of it other than to a collector. We were not to put salvage in the dustbin or mix it with any other rubbish. One local couple appeared in court for refusing to separate their rubbish as *'it was against their conscience to help manufacture weapons'*. At school we were told to use every inch of the pages in our exercise books, including margins. Gummed economy labels were introduced as a means of using envelopes more than once, and paper bags and tissue paper for wrapping loaves, disappeared from the shops. Shopping baskets became the standard container for bringing home the food.

Many tenants of property in Hastings had, on government advice, gone to live elsewhere in the country, leaving their homes just as they were. Subsequently, they fell into arrears with rent and rates. To help ease the situation, a moratorium was declared on such payments. This arrangement gave rise to much trouble and confusion. As the months went by, arrears built up and landlords began to go to court to reclaim possession of their property. The courts were faced with a dilemma. On the one hand they had a landlord who could not afford to do without his rent: on the other, a tenant who had left the town, and could not pay. A legal ruling was given that tenants were excused payment in the short term, but would eventually have to pay up. They were advised to pay whatever they could meanwhile, and so avoid building up massive arrears.

From 15th February, the ban on entry to the town, except on business, was re-imposed.

Friday, 24th April

Two Messerschmitt 109s crossed the coast in cloud. They swept round to the back of the town, then, with guns blazing, dropped two large H.E. bombs as they made their way out to sea. One fell on the West Hill close to the lift damaging houses in George Street. The other demolished three houses in Wellington Road. There were a number of casualties, three of them serious.

Sunday, 3rd May.

Five people were killed, 12 seriously injured, and 23 others hurt in a particularly tragic raid by four Messerschmitt 109 fighter bombers. One tiny victim of the attack was the infant daughter of the Reverend Battersby, vicar of Emmanuel Church in Vicarage Road. The Church was damaged, but the adjoining vicarage received a direct hit. The little girl who was asleep in her cot was buried in the ruins. Another of the bombs fell right in the centre of Emmanuel Road, setting light to a gas main, and sending flames leaping into the air. Windows on either side of the street were blown in. Several people were killed, one man was blinded by flying glass, and many others seriously cut. A young eyewitness said, 'We lived high up in a flat in St George's Road which had a glorious view over the town from the rear windows. It was a beautiful place from which to watch the sunsets, and an ideal vantage point for plane spotting. Around nine o'clock on the evening of the attack, I happened to be looking out, when I heard and saw four planes coming over The Ridge from the top of Elphinstone Road. There had been no air-raid warning, and I expected them to be British fighters of some sort. They were very low down, very close together, and were flying straight towards me, as though they were about to come in the window. As they got close, they swooped slightly upwards and fanned apart. At that moment and to my horror, instead of the RAF roundels, I saw black crosses under the wings. In the same second, I saw a bomb falling from each of the two leading planes. I shouted "bombs" to my

Vicarage of Emmanuel Church, destroyed on Sunday, 3rd May 1942.

parents, who were in the same room, and we all dived to the floor. There were two almighty explosions which shook the house, and then two more further away. My father, a police officer off duty, grabbed his tin helmet and rushed out. We didn't see him again until the early hours. He had spent most of his time at the Vicarage helping to shift the debris. The vicar was away at the time, but his wife, who was injured, waited anxiously while the men worked. The vicar's little daughter was eventually found dead among the wreckage. We thought afterwards that the pilots had used the Church tower as a target, as it was so prominent on the skyline'.

German pilot's-eye view of Emmanuel Church, Priory Road – a prominent landmark used as a target by 'hit and run' raiders.

In that same attack the other bombs fell in Oakfield Road and Ore, where two sisters were buried in their shop. They were extricated from the ruins around midnight. Both were dead.

Sunday, 17th May.

Another four M.E. 109s attacked two weeks later, at lunch time, when bombs fell in Havelock Road, Middle Street, Falaise Road and the sea. These were followed by machine-gunning. At a house in St George's Road, a young mother, aged 28, was attending to her baby in an upstairs room. A machine gun bullet smashed through the window striking her in the chest causing massive bleeding from which she died shortly afterwards. The baby was taken to hospital with lacerations.

Tuesday, 2nd June.

Early in the morning, two British fighters were returning home from across the channel. Their victory roll, as they flew low over the town, indicated that they were in good spirits. Tragically, they collided with one another and crashed, one on allotments behind Parker Road, the other in Hoad's Wood Road. Both pilots, from 81st Squadron, RAF Hornchurch, were killed.

Many 'Tip and Run' raids were carried out at great speed all along the coast, before the regional alert could be sounded. Those in charge of Civil Defence felt that Hastings should have its own warning system, which could be quickly operated. In another attempt to ensure greater safety, and as there had been many deaths from falling masonry, we were all urged to obtain a steel Morrison Table Shelter from the Council. These could be installed inside the house and gave good protection.

One of the many posters which appeared in public places warned us that 'CARELESS TALK COSTS LIVES'. It was also an offence to 'spread alarm and despondency'. The newly arrived Chief Constable, Mr Angus Cargill, found it necessary to interview two people who had publicly made unfounded statements of an alarmist nature. He gave them firm advice on the subject of spreading rumours and said that, in future cases, prosecution would follow.

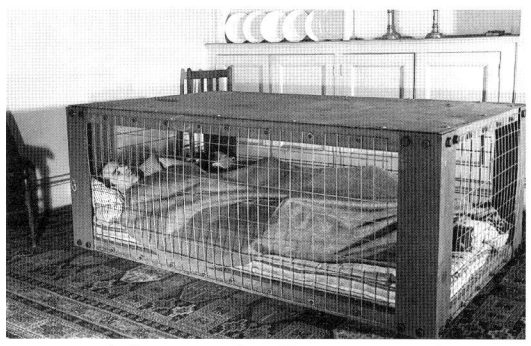

Morrison Shelter. (Reproduced by permission of the Imperial War Museum)

Because of the re-imposition of the ban on visitors to the defence area, the town was without its normal summer visitors. On the strangely quiet August Bank Holiday weekend, unauthorised visitors to the town were turned back by police who kept a strict check on main roads into the town, and at rail and coach stations. Local people, who were free from their war-time duties, spent time at the cinemas or at the swimming baths. Two events at the White Rock Pavilion were completely sold out. The RAF Dance Band came to give a concert on Sunday, at which there was standing room only, and on Monday, the same band provided music for a dance, which was so packed that many were turned away.

Saturday, August 22nd.

Two F.W. 190s bombed Boyne Road and Berlin Road causing 36 casualties, 12 of them serious. There was the usual accompaniment of cannon fire.

In late August, on a more rustic note, a party of police officers gave up their rest days to travel to Robertsbridge. With their wives and families, they set about helping to harvest the corn.

rged to restrict our bath water to a depth of five inches in order
and fuel. To further that aim, the Council offered to replace any
hers free of charge. In another measure to save materials, all
ery, or other unnecessary decoration were banned from
alls. Expectant mothers were given an additional 60 coupons
for the new baby's needs.

Monday, 21st September

In another raid, two bombs fell on St Leonards. The two top storeys of Marine Court were damaged. Fortunately, the building was largely unoccupied except for staff.

Thursday, 24th September

Seven fighter-bombers with an escort of fighters, again attacked St Leonards in the afternoon. The Royal National Institute for the Blind Home at Quarry Hill was hit. Two of the blind residents were killed, and several injured, including the Matron. The Chief Constable attended and spent hours, with the rescue squads, helping to reach the victims. Other bombs fell in Warrior Square, West Hill, and De Cham Road. The high blast effect of the powerful bombs caused many tall Victorian buildings to crumble, burying many victims. There was a death toll of 23 in this raid, with 64 injured of whom 21 were seriously hurt. The injured included a number of Service casualties.

Saturday, 17th October

Two people were killed, eight seriously injured, and eight others hurt when bombs from two FW 190s fell at lunch time. St Columbus Church, houses in Pevensey Road, and a warehouse in Warrior Gardens were wrecked. In that incident, Mr Sydney Oak, a C.D. Rescue Party Leader, showed great bravery at a house in Pevensey Road. Three people had been trapped in the debris. Two were rescued in daylight, but as night fell, hope began to fade for the third person, but they carried on. In the early hours, a woman's faint cry was

House in Pevensey Road, bombed on 17th October 1942. Mr Sydney Oak was awarded the George Medal for his great courage in rescuing an occupant.

heard. With the help of Mr F Coleman, Mr Oak made a tunnel in the wreckage. He crawled in to comfort the woman and cover her face from the falling dust. There was imminent danger of a further collapse, but he remained there for two hours until the others reached them. Mr Oak was later awarded the George Medal *'For great courage and devotion to duty'*.

The now famous Dieppe Raid took place on 19th August 1942. In October, people living in the coastal area received a government leaflet about the possibility of similar retaliatory raids by the Germans. We were told that, if possible, a warning would be given by loudspeaker cars announcing 'ENEMY LANDING RAID - TAKE COVER'. We were to take shelter and remain there until told that the raid was over.

In the same month, the sharp-eyed Food Office staff were once again quick to spot irregularities from a retailer. This time, it involved 'points' used for tinned goods, and 'personal points' used for the sweet ration. In all, the offences involved quantities sufficient for one month's rations for 130 people. The offender was fined £20, and allowed to pay at £1 per week.

Monday, 26th October

A persistent lone Junkers 88 bomber made several approaches to drop its bombs. Faced with a heavy AA barrage, it twice turned away out to sea. On the third attempt, it braved the guns to drop its bombs on High Beech Estate, causing damage and one casualty.

In November, at Summerfields, the wartime home of the Town Hall, councillors complained bitterly, and at length, about the temperature in the Council Chamber. The building was likened to a refrigerator, and councillors sat in overcoats and gloves. The Town Clerk explained that the boiler had been condemned by the Insurance Company, and although attempts were being made to get it repaired it was not given priority. He went on to say, rather unsympathetically, that he had to endure those conditions all the time. The incident served to illustrate the difficulties of getting maintenance jobs attended to during wartime.

On Sunday, 5th November, a joyous sound was heard for the first time since 'The great Silence' had been imposed on church bells in 1940. With others throughout the land, the bells of St Clement's Church rang out once more in celebration of our recent victory at the Battle of El Alamein, in North Africa. This was the first really good news the country had received for a long time, and it certainly gladdened our hearts to hear the pealing of the bells.

Later in that month, another event that gave great pleasure was the 'Dig for Victory Exhibition' at the White Rock Pavilion. The Lower Hall looked and smelled like an enormous harvest festival as local people proudly displayed the results of their labours. Fruit, vegetables, preserves and even rabbits were all exhibited, and awards were made for the best in various classes.

In December, a booklet entitled 'Front Line' 1940-1941 was issued by the Ministry of Information. The following figures show how Hastings compared with nearby towns in those two years.

Town	Raids	Killed	Houses Damaged
Bexhill	37	74	2,600
Brighton & Hove	25	127	4,500
Eastbourne	49	36	3,700
Hastings	40	46	6,200

Week ending 12th December

The year of the 'Hit and Run' raids ended as it had begun, with machine-gunning. Sedlescombe Road North, Bulverhythe Road and Bexhill Road were all targeted, but the single bomber caused no damage or casualties.

15
THE MOUNTING TOLL

There was no respite as 1943 opened. The machine gunning continued, and the Luftwaffe began to use bigger bombs and more planes in the raids.

Monday, 4th January

Just four days into the New Year, three members of the Women's Land Army were machine gunned as they worked in fields near the town. Three planes were involved. One was brought down by anti-aircraft fire, got entangled in telephone wires and burst into flames. A second plane was also destroyed. The third was pursued by fighters.

Saturday, 9th January

A hit-and-run raider dropped bombs at Mill Lane and at The White Hart Inn, Guestling. An 80-year-old woman, her daughter and their maid, were all killed by a direct hit on their house.

Sunday, 17th January

Bombs fell on the eastern edge of the town near Fairlight Place and Tilekiln Cottage, off Fairlight Road.

Wednesday, 20th January

A large formation of bombers approached the town. They were seen off by heavy AA fire and British fighters. Bexhill Road was once again in the firing line but escaped with just damaged roofs.

Queen Victoria's Statue in Warrior Square, showing bullet hole in her skirt.

Thursday, 28th January

Glyne Gap gasworks (now the Ravenside shopping centre) were attacked by two fighter-bombers. Several employees suffered serious injuries, one of whom died later in hospital.

Tuesday, 9th February

Raiders dropped 2,000-pound bombs, one of which demolished most of St John's Church in Pevensey Road, and its adjoining parish room. Other bombs of the same size fell at Ashbrook Road, Hollington, but failed to explode. At Ore, 14 smaller bombs fell, damaging Christ Church and causing damage in Moscow Road and Alfred Road. Three people were killed on that day, three seriously injured and two others hurt.

Monday, 13th February

Mr Robert Willey, a local engine driver for Southern Railway became something of a hero whilst on his way to London with a trainload of commuters. It was still partly dark when the train was attacked by cannon fire from an enemy plane. Knowing there was a tunnel not far ahead, Mr Willey put on speed to reach it. Once inside, he slowed down and emerged with great caution at the other end. The train arrived in London with a number of bullet holes, but no casualties.

Later that month, Hastings was at last given a local warning system of its own. Bells were installed in such schools as had been re-opened. Private schools were also included in the scheme. The arrangement came not a moment too soon as, a couple of weeks later, the town was to have its worst raid of the whole war.

Thursday, 11th March

Ten F.W. 190s and about ten M.E. 109s. brought death and destruction to the town. They came over in waves at roof-top level so that the bombs fell at a shallow angle to the ground, often with strange effect. At the Police Station house in Battle Road, an officer was asleep upstairs. A bomb came through the back of the building, passed over his bed and burst through the front wall of the bedroom, before exploding behind the Tivoli Tavern in Adelaide Road. Although Silverhill and the adjoining Bohemia area were the worst affected, the 500-kilo H.E. bombs, numbering 25 in all, were widely scattered. A total of 38 people were killed, 39 seriously injured, and 51 others hurt.

Silverhill Junction showing parade of shops destroyed by a direct hit on 11th March 1943.

A pupil at Barton, a small private school in Sedlescombe Road South, recalls, *'We were all hard at work one afternoon, when, for the first time, the* warning bell rang in the hall. Knowing that it signalled immediate danger, we hurried to our places of shelter. The girls took refuge under the large staircase on the ground floor. The boys made for the kitchen at the back of the house which had been reinforced with large balks of timber. We had just got there, when we heard the planes, and then bombs started to fall. It was deafening and terrifying. The house shook as bombs exploded, and nearby anti-aircraft guns started pounding away. We could hear the little ones upstairs crying with fright. At one point, the house gave a violent shudder. The racket seemed to go on for ages, but finally, everything went quiet. We emerged from our places of refuge with our ears ringing as we tried to recover our wits. The Headmistress gathered us all together, checked that no-one was hurt, and then sent us home. With some other girls, I walked along Sedlescombe Road South towards Silverhill junction. We heard ambulance and fire engine bells clanging as we walked. As we got closer, the first thing we saw was Sayer's the drapers at the corner of Battle Road (now a bank). Its windows had been smashed and all the slates were missing. The whole of the junction was a scene of devastation and activity. There were ambulances, fire engines, police and rescue workers everywhere. The whole of the road surface was covered with broken slates, glass and other debris. The parade of shops, which all had their living accommodation above, had suffered a direct hit from a massive bomb. Shops belonging to Love the grocer, Sargent the ironmonger, Gower the tobacconist, Nye the fruiterer, and Gregory the Baker, were just piles of rubble. Potter's the second-hand shop was half in ruins. The parents of one of my classmates kept the tobacconist's shop. We heard the next day that her father had been killed, and her mother rescued from the wreckage, seriously injured. I picked my way through the debris on my way to Vale Road, where we lived. As I

House on the corner of Combermere Road/Springfield Road destroyed on 11th March 1943. The bomb 'bounced' over from a nearby garden.

passed the end of Strood Road, I saw that St Matthew's School, fortunately not in use, and some of the houses next to it had been flattened. Further on, I saw between the houses on my left, that another bomb had fallen in Alma Terrace just behind our house. My heart was thumping all the way as I hurried down the road, wondering whether my mother and our house would still be there. When I reached home, which thankfully was still intact, apart from some *broken windows, collapsed ceilings and missing slates, I found my mother in the back kitchen quietly drinking tea with an elderly man, who lived nearby. She just glanced at me and said, "Oh, so you're all right then". I think her seemingly calm air was meant to give the neighbour, who was visibly shaking, the impression that there was not a lot to worry about. Later that evening we were told that a bomb was sticking out of the ground in the back garden of my school, about ten feet from the boys' shelter. It turned out to be just the fin. The bomb itself had bounced and exploded on a house at the corner of Combermere and Springfield Road, killing the occupant."*

The damage to property was enormous on that occasion. Many people were buried under the debris, and rescue work went on all that night and for some time afterwards, not only at Silverhill, but at many other places in the town. Soldiers, quartered in the town, joined with the rescue services to recover victims from the demolished houses. Some of the dead were not found for two or three days, but there is no doubt that the Morrison table-shelters proved their worth. One was blown right out of a house into the garden with an elderly lady still inside it. The shelter landed upside down, but she emerged unharmed, except for shock. Rest centres filled a great need in accommodating the many homeless, and mobile canteens provided food and drink for the rescuers during their protracted work

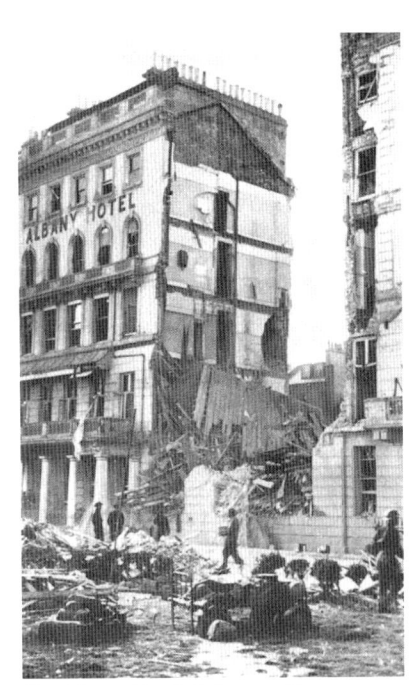

The Albany Hotel, Robertson Terrace, 23rd May 1943.

Sunday, 23rd May

This, the second heaviest raid on Hastings, killed 25 people, and injured another 85, 30 of them seriously. This time it was a large group of F.W.s which swept low along the front line from east to west dropping 25 large H.E. bombs and unleashing machine gun fire as they went. It was 1.0 p.m. when most pubs, of which five were hit, were full of people. Many of the hotels on the sea front were being used to house Canadian troops. The 7th Canadian Reconnaissance Regiment of the Royal Canadian Hussars were quartered in the terrace of hotels at Carlisle Parade. They had arrived in the town on 6th May from Brighton where a lot of them had helped with rescue work in raids there. On May 19th, just four days before the raid, the men had proudly taken part in the Hastings 'Wings for Victory' parade through the town. Sadly, about ten days later, eleven of them were to be driven through the same streets, in coffins, as part of a regimental funeral. The 23rd May was fine and sunny, and men were relaxing on the lawn in front of the hotels whilst waiting for lunch. The Albany Hotel (now rebuilt as Albany Court flats) was being used as the officers' mess. Disaster came without warning when it was demolished by a bomb which first passed through the top of the nearby Queen's Hotel. Eleven men were killed, and 34 injured.

The same raid caused a similar scene of destruction in the Old Town when the Swan Hotel, in the High Street, received a direct hit. The place was crowded with customers and others who had hurried inside on hearing the planes. Only one man and a dog survived. Rescue work went on throughout the night and all of the next day. Among the dead were the Licensee's wife and 3-year-old child, Mr William Hilder, the lifeboat mechanic, and a local police officer's six-year-old daughter who had been out with her aunt. In St Leonards, the Warrior House Hotel received a direct hit. Wreckage of The Warrior Gate public House on the corner of Norman Road caught fire following a direct hit. The Tower Hotel in Bohemia had a lucky escape when a bomb fell through the cellar flap but failed to explode. On that occasion the AA guns put up a strong defence, and fighters chased the raiders back out to sea.

Ruins of the Swan Hotel, High Street, after raid on Sunday, 23rd May 1943.

Friday, July 9th

St Leonards was again the target when a single bomber dropped 14 bombs over a wide area. There was considerable damage to property including two four-storey houses in Markwick Terrace. There was one serious casualty.

On Wednesday, 8th September, we all heard some welcome news. In the 6 o'clock bulletin, the BBC announced the Italian surrender. The news quickly spread throughout the town, and a few extra pints were downed that evening.

The general feeling of relief was tempered by the knowledge that the Italians were not the worst of our foes, and we still had a long way to go to win the war.

At the end of October, several Hastings families received word that their men, who were prisoners of war, had been selected for repatriation. The men had been wounded earlier in the war, and were being released on medical grounds. They had a circuitous journey home via Gothenburg in Sweden, where they were looked after very well, before embarking for the Scottish port of Leith on their way home to Hastings. They spoke of the low German morale after their enormous losses on the Russian front at Stalingrad, and their failure to reach Moscow. Their general impression was that many Germans felt they had already lost the war. All the men recorded their gratitude for the Red Cross parcels which reached them in captivity, and to which they owed their survival. The repatriated men were entertained to a special 'Welcome Home' evening by the local branch of the British Legion.

Removing UX bomb from the Tower Hotel, Tower Road, after raid on 23rd May 1943.

Surprisingly, there was one woman with the men who returned to Hastings. This was a Miss Brigham who, before the outbreak of war, had been travelling in Europe with her sister. Her sister returned home but she remained in Paris. In December 1940, after the German occupation of France, she was rounded up with other foreigners, and interned. She too, expressed her thanks for the arrival of Red Cross parcels which *'kept body and soul together'*.

By the end of the year, there was a lightening of mood, both nationally and locally. In local council meetings, this optimism was shown by the positive discussion of post-war plans for the town. Among the general population, in spite of the disastrous air-raids that year, the hardships of rationing and general shortages of goods in the shops, there was hope. This was engendered by the German debacle in Russia, the Italian surrender, the safe return of some of our men, and the gradual fading of the fear that the Germans might land on our beaches.

16
BEFORE AND AFTER D-DAY

The mood in Hastings at the start 1944 was one of confidence. In Council circles, officials were clearly optimistic that the war would end before long. There were discussions about a new college for the post-war education of the town's young people. Concerns were expressed over the state of St Leonards Golf Course. It was said that the cattle grazing there were ruining it, and much restoration work would have to be done. The general feeling was that golf would be played there again sooner rather than later. Among the general public there was no doubt that Britain would win the war. It was just a question of when.

Wednesday, 5th January

Just a few days into the new year, Hastings suffered a great loss. Mr David Ligat, an eminent surgeon was, at the age of 72, continuing with his work in the local hospitals. He was returning to his house in Filsham Road in the early hours, having just performed an emergency operation at the Royal East Sussex Hospital. As he got out of his car a bomb exploded outside the house. A firewatcher on the house opposite was killed by a splinter, and Mr Ligat's right arm was blown off. His wife found him outside, and he was rushed back to the hospital he had just left. He advised his colleagues on the treatment he received and remarked wryly, *'Well that's finished my golf'*.

In February 1944, a subject relevant to Hastings was under discussion in the House of Commons. It concerned the problems arising out of the creation of the coastal Defence Area. The situation was summed up very well by Sir Robert Gower who said, *'. . . the area has been subject to quite exceptional conditions. No other part of the country has been taken over to the same extent for military defence. In consequence, the whole life of many towns has been disrupted and Treasury aid has had to be sought. Evacuation had been advised with such official earnestness that it was treated as actual instructions. Visitors had been banned, and Moratoria had only caused an accumulation of debt to be faced later on. A great many people had been deprived of their livelihood, and to a large extent local life was dead'*. He went on to say that help should be given to individuals as well as to Local Authorities. A government committee was set up to examine the problems of the area.

St Leonards Palace Pier, which had been a source of pleasure to so many people in pre-war days, was severely damaged by fire on 7th March. Flames were visible for miles along the coast, but the Fire Service succeeded in controlling the fire before black-out time, around 7.30 p.m.

Sunday, 12th March

The town lost a well-known member of its community in another raid. Mr Leslie Badham, a gifted artist and teacher at Hastings School of Art, died in hospital after being rescued from the ruins of his house in Priory Road, opposite Emmanuel Church. His daughter also died in hospital, although his wife survived serious injuries. Three other people were killed and Emmanuel Church was again damaged.

Monday, 27th March

The last conventional H.E. bomb to fall on the town was dropped in Filsham Road at 11.50 p.m. It damaged houses on both sides of the road and injured two people.

For some time there had been talk of a 'Second Front'. This was to take the form of an Allied invasion of Europe in a concerted attempt to drive the Germans out of all the countries they had been dominating since 1939. It was just a question of time. For long months, men in khaki, army convoys, bren-gun carriers and other assorted military vehicles had been a common sight on the streets of Hastings. Along with the rest of the South of England, the town had been home to thousands of British and Canadian troops waiting for the moment to embark. They were quartered in requisitioned hotels on the seafront, and in a good many of the larger private houses elsewhere in the town. In the Cricket Ground troops were seen undergoing 'bayonet practice'. Screaming like men possessed, they would run at a sack stuffed with straw suspended from a frame, and thrust their bayonets into it. For the children of the town it was good free, if blood-curdling, entertainment. In the Silverhill area, groups of soldiers from Hollington Park would set off each morning on route marches. Striding out briskly, in full kit, they would head out of the town, only to trudge back later in the day, obviously weary. It was not made public at the time, but they were being toughened up in preparation for the forthcoming invasion of Europe.

On 1st April a new coastal security area was announced. 10 miles in depth, it stretched from the Wash to Land's End. This was commonly supposed to be in preparation for the 'Second Front' and penalties of £100 or 3

Coastal Security Area imposed on 1st April 1944 in preparation for D-Day.

months imprisonment were imposed on anyone entering the area without permission. Those living within the zone were forbidden to use telescopes or binoculars. At a special talk and film show at the Ritz cinema, Civil Defence workers and others were reminded of the dangers of careless talk. They were told the enemy was particularly interested in the 2nd Front, and were instructed to keep quiet about anything they knew.

The prospects of a good summer season vanished overnight. Rating records for the year showed that there were 669 empty or non-operative shops in the town, and trade was at a very low ebb. The only 'visitors' in the town were the masses of troops who helped to keep the public houses ticking over when supplies of drink permitted. On May 12th, Winston Churchill inspected invasion forces at the Pilot Field and gave an address. He was accompanied by General Smuts, PM of South Africa, and McKenzie King, PM of Canada.

As preparations for the start of the 2nd Front advanced, the khaki-clad visitors began to disappear from our streets.

Throughout the night of June 5th/6th, the roar of hundreds of planes passing over the town was heard. At dawn, watchers with 'forbidden' binoculars saw a great invasion fleet steaming down the channel. It therefore came as no surprise to anyone to hear, on the early news bulletin, that a great armada of ships and landing craft had, with air and naval upport, crossed the Channel and disembarked the Allied armies at various points along the coast of Normandy. D-Day had arrived: Operation Overlord had begun. For the rest of that day, most people kept their radio sets switched on to catch any news flashes. The news on subsequent days was good. The first wave of invasion troops had established bridgeheads, and were pressing on with their task. The end of the war was in sight, and Hastings dreamed of assuming once more its peacetime role.

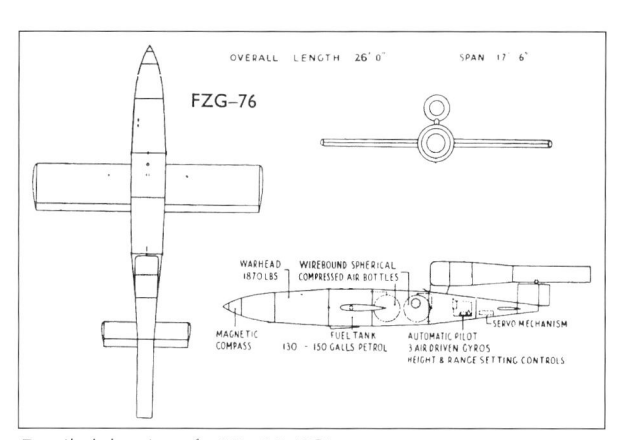

Detailed drawing of a V1. (HMSO).

One week later, rudely awakened from the dream of peace, the south-east coast found itself once more in the front line. In a last desperate attempt at revenge, Hitler had decided to unleash his secret weapon, the V1 flying bomb. This devilish device, which carried 1,870 lbs of explosive, was in the form of a small pilotless aircraft. It also went by the name of Robot, Buzz Bomb or Doodle Bug. To the Germans it was Vergeltungswaffe, or retaliation weapon. The launching ramps were scattered in woodland in numerous places throughout northern France, from where the bombs were directed to fall on London. The first one to cross the English coast was spotted by two members of the Observer Corps at Dymchurch in Kent, on 13th June 1944.

Friday, 16th June

The first bomb to pass over Hastings was heard shortly before midnight on 15th June. At first, the strange noise and flames coming from its rear, caused people to think it was an ordinary plane 'in trouble'. However, when the same thing was repeated throughout a twelve-hour alert, watchers realised it was something different. In the morning, it was said that these were flying bombs, and that one had been brought down by AA gunfire at Glyne Gap early that day. It exploded violently on the seaward side of the railway line near the Bull Inn, shattering windows, stripping tiles from roofs and blowing doors off their hinges. Extra AA guns arrived between July and September and were placed at strategic points around the town. Their task was to bring down the bombs and prevent them from reaching London. The crew of one battery on the West Hill included Winston Churchill's daughter, Mary, who was billeted in a house in Collier Road.

Throughout the next few months flying bombs were launched day and night, and the never-to-be-forgotten roar of their approach was a daily occurence. The noise of the AA guns pounding away, and the rattle of fighters attacking them, became nerve-racking and frightening elements of daily life. There were six flight paths directly over the town and it was estimated that of all the

Anti-aircraft guns at Grosvenor Crescent, St Leonards-on-Sea.

bombs directed at London, 40% crossed the coast between Rye and Bexhill. People living directly under a flight path, were advised to arrange with friends elsewhere in the town to go to them if they were bombed out. In all 15 V1s fell within the Borough. Four people were killed, 29 seriously injured, 87 others hurt and property damaged. Many bombs fell on open ground causing few casualties.

The younger people of the town took great delight in watching British and American fighters chasing the bombs. The object was to avoid bringing them down on the town and consequently Battle Rural District had 374 bombs fall in its area.

Tuesday, 11th July

John Kennett, who was at home in Burry Road with Michael, his twin brother, recalls, *'It was lunch time on this particular day. Father was at work in the town, and mother was working at the RASC records office. We had just finished lunch when we heard the unmistakable pulsing engine sound of a doodlebug approaching. We rushed outside into the back garden, more out of curiosity than concern, since we could hear that the engine was still running, taking the missile away from the town. It was a bright sunny day. We could clearly see the bomb approaching at about 800ft, pursued by two Spitfires and an American Thunderbolt. The Thunderbolt was overtaking the Spitfires and, to our astonishment, it opened fire. This was alarming for two reasons: firstly it appeared that the British aircraft were in the line of fire and, secondly, we knew that when a doodlebug's engine stopped it usually went into a descending left turn, and this would have brought it extremely close to us. In the event, the American hit the target with his second burst. I remember we reacted by lying flat on the ground. In fact the bomb went $^1/_2$ mile further on before exploding'.*

Damage at Hollington from a V1 brought down by fighters.

This incident occurred at 12.45 p.m. The bomb exploded in an orchard near Meophams Bank (Ledsham Avenue area) in Sedlescombe Road North.

Sunday, 16th July

There was a more serious incident when a V1 was again brought down by fighters. It fell in Old Church Road, Hollington, killing three people, and injuring 47 others.

Thursday, 20th July

The last person to die in Hastings from enemy bombs was a woman. She was killed at Shearbarn Farmhouse, on the East Hill, when it was damaged by a V1 which crashed in a nearby field.

Saturday, 29th July

St Leonards Parish Church and neighbouring houses on the sea-front were destroyed at 11.40 p.m. when a V1 came in very low over the sea, passed over the railings and exploded on the front steps of the church.

Pieces of the last flying bomb destroyed over the town fell harmlessly in Battle Road and Old Harrow Road on August 2nd. Thereafter, as the launching sites in northern France were overrun by the Allied advance towards Germany, so the number of V1s roaring over Hastings gradually became less until, finally, they ceased and the guns fell silent.

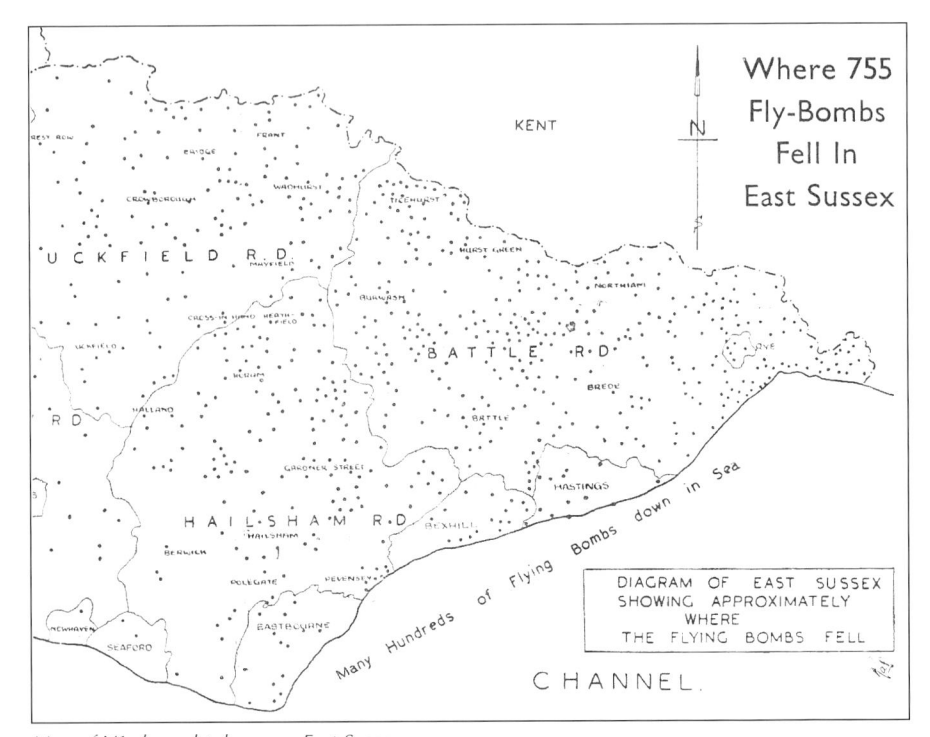

Map of V1s brought down on East Sussex.

On Friday, August 25th, amid great rejoicing, the Allied armies reached and liberated Paris. On the very same day the War Office announce the lifting of both the coastal ban and the curfew. This also brought a warning that the easing did not mean the coast was free from all enemy attacks and missiles. In spite of that, the announcement was hailed as the best news for Hastings in a long time. There was a call for all barbed wire in the town to come down. Incoming trains on the next two days brought throngs of visitors to the town. They were able to enjoy a day at the seaside for the first time in years. They brought their sandwiches and watched the preparations for re-opening the lower promenade and beach.

On Tuesday, 29th August, the beach was re-opened to the public. From a store where they had been locked away since 1940, deckchairs were brought out into the light of day in perfect condition, and fit for immediate use. Shortly afterwards, the Borough Electrical Engineer set about restoring street lamps in preparation for 'victory lights'. *'We don't want to be caught napping',* he said.

From September 17th, the Chief Constable authorised an easing of the black-out. 'Half window' lighting was allowed with the proviso that if an alert sounded, full black-out was to be reinstated. Clearing of all remaining barbed wire continued apace, and road blocks dating from 1940 were removed. The government earmarked £5,000,000 to help stricken resorts, the first 12 street lamps were switched on around the memorial, and Hastings felt it had taken the first steps towards a brighter future.

The local Grammar School had been evacuated to St Albans for over four years. Host families who, in 1940, had willingly opened their homes to the boys, had lost their initial enthusiasm. On several occasions, the boys' parents had asked for the school to be re-opened in Hastings, only to meet delaying tactics both from the govenors and the LEA. In October, the parents' patience finally came to an end, and a minor rebellion took place. Over a hundred

A warning to would-be thieves.

parents met at the the Central Hall, and signed a pledge not to send their boys back to St Albans after the autumn half-term holiday. They vowed to send them instead to the school premises in Nelson Road. Thus, the Governing body had its hand forced, and a decision was made to re-open the school immediately.

In the same month, St Clement's Caves, which had served as an air-raid shelter since 1940, were officially closed. Throughout the Battle of Britain up to 900 people had lived, eaten and slept there. They had been extensively used during the 'hit and run' raids, and when the new menace of Flying Bombs posed a daily threat to life and limb, the Caves again proved a safe refuge for great numbers of people. The decision to close them gave proof, if any were needed, that the dangers the town had faced for so long had finally passed.

Throughout all the bombing attacks on Hastings, there were 1467 air-raid warnings and more than 100 cuckoo alerts. On 9th November 1944, the air-raid siren sounded for the last time and in the same month it was announced that the Home Guard would stand down on 3rd December. There was a final parade of 500 men of whom the oldest was ex-Sergeant-Major Crouch, aged 74.

During December, when it became clear that, for all practical purposes, remaining evacuees need no longer stay away in the reception areas, large numbers of them returned to the town. Sadly, and to the shame of those responsible, many families found their homes looted, damaged and in some cases uninhabitable. Bedding and mattresses had either been stolen or were so damp that further use was impossible. Crockery, furniture and utensils had disappeared, and as all these items were either rationed or largely unobtainable, there were severe problems. Nevertheless, Christmas 1944 was the brightest since the war began. The sun shone, visitors flocked to the town and all available accommodation was booked up.

17
SUNSHINE

Following D-Day, Hastings lost the majority of its 'military guests' who had been occupying requisitioned hotels and boarding houses. The government had been paying rent to the owners of such premises. It was now possible to apply for 'derequisitioning' as, by the beginning of 1945, the town was looking forward to peace, and the resumption of its normal role as a holiday resort. There was one great problem standing in the way. After several years of occupation by the military, the hotels needed renovating and refurbishing before holiday-makers could again be accommodated. If derequisitioning were granted, the rent would stop, and owners would face the lengthy task of restoring the premises without any income. Understandably, many owners were reluctant to apply without knowing how they would bridge the gap. Hastings Council discussed how best to safeguard the situation. Questions were asked at national level, and the response was that an honorarium, equivalent to one year's rent, would be paid once derequisitioning was granted.

Food rationing continued to cause problems for the hard-pressed housewives. Although restaurant meals were 'off ration' ordinary families could not afford these very often. Fish and chip shops provided a cheap alternative, but only opened sporadically when fish was available. Many a hungry teenager trekked from shop to shop in the hope of finding some supper, only to return home disappointed and even more hungry. Happily, British Restaurants came to the rescue. At the Tower Road School Restaurant, a very good mid-day meal could be bought for 1/- (5p), and an extra old penny or two would buy a dessert. A typical meal would be a main course of a delicious bacon and egg flan. Quiche was an unknown word then, and the flan was made with dried eggs. The dessert might be simply plain boiled rice with a spoonful of jam, but as the saying goes, 'hunger is the best sauce'.

The National Service Regulations, which came into force at the beginning of the war, continued to be applied with vigour. The following account illustrates the restrictions under which civilian workers lived. Three local women who, when the war started, had a boarding house in the town, volunteered for war work and were directed to jobs at Kings Cross Station where they worked as porters. The work was hard and often involved shifting heavy loads from wagons to vans. They did this work for three and a half years. When the ban on entry to the defence zone was lifted, they applied for release and then returned to Hastings to re-open their boarding house. Unfortunately, there was a delay in processing their application, which they thought was just a formality. Early in 1945, they were taken to court 'for leaving their work without permission'.

Every tenth man called up for National Service was selected to work in the coal mines. In February there was the first prosecution in Hastings for refusing to report as directed.

On 14th April, Hastings Council held its last meeting at Summerfields Preparatory School, the wartime home of the Town Clerk's department.

Ever since D-Day we had eagerly followed the progress of the Allied armies. Their advance was checked during December 1944 and January 1945 by the sub-zero temperatures and by the German counter offensive in the Ardennes. With the return of Spring, came the final push towards Berlin. Then, on May 1st, like a bolt from the blue, BBC radio programmes were interrupted and the announcer, Stuart Hibberd, said, *'This is London calling. Here is a news flash. The German radio has just announced that Hitler is dead.'* Unable to bear defeat, he had shot himself in Berlin as the Allied and Russian armies closed in. Unashamedly, the people of Hastings greeted the news with cheering and set about celebrating Hitler's demise. The next few days were spent in joyful anticipation of further good tidings. Would the Germans now surrender or would they still try to fight without their leader?

The war ended in agonisingly slow steps. First the Germans in Italy surrendered on 2nd May. Later that evening another news flash gave the news that Berlin had fallen. Two days later the German troops in Denmark surrendered. The waiting was unbearable. Everyone knew the war was over but still there was no official announcement. Radios were kept tuned to catch any news flashes. Finally, on the evening of 7th May, John Snagge's familiar voice was heard, *'This is the BBC Home Service. We are interrupting programmes to make the following announcement. It is understood that in accordance with arrangements between the three great powers, an official announcement will be broadcast by the Prime Minister at 3 o'clock tomorrow, Tuesday afternoon, the 8th May.'* Winston Churchill duly obliged. In Hastings people turned the volume up on their radios, and left their windows open so that passers-by could hear his words, *'Yesterday at 2.41 a.m. the representatives of the German High Command signed the act of unconditional surrender of all German land, sea, and air forces in Europe'.* He went on, in true Churchillian style, to refer to Hitler's *'foul aggression'* and to *'the evil doers, now prostrate before us'.* He told us that May 8th and 9th were to be celebrated as Victory in Europe days.

We needed no telling. Bunting and flags, unearthed from stores, attics and cupboards, were already decorating the town. That morning, the Fire Brigade had risen early, bringing their ladders, to bedeck the Memorial area. Cars were decorated, buses had streamers flying from them, and suddenly the drab war-time town was awash with colour. The Town Hall balcony was draped with flags and the Mayor, Alderman A Blackman, came out to address a large crowd of townspeople who cheered and applauded with unrestrained joy. Church services were held to give thanks for our deliverance, and everywhere there were smiling faces and a feeling of great relief. On Wednesday evening, 9th May, the Old Town celebrated as only it knew how. In a carnival atmosphere, dense crowds gathered round Winkle Island where the Harmony Aces' band played for dancing. The fishermen strung bunting from the masts of their boats, a huge bonfire blazed on the beach at Rock-a-Nore, and army thunderflashes served as makeshift fireworks. Young and old alike laughed, sang and danced on air late into the night. They went wild with joy as the weight of six years of war was lifted from their shoulders.

War Memorial in Alexandra Park where salute was taken by the Mayor during the Victory Parade on 13th May 1945.

Street parties were arranged for the children, notably one in Priory Street. At that time, it was a little used street lined with small cottages on both sides, and trestle tables were set out containing a surprising array of goodies.

On the following Sunday, 13th May, Hastings added the final chapter to the annals of its part in the war with Germany. Church bells rang out joyously for many hours throughout the town. In the afternoon, Army Units, RAF personnel, the ATS, Home Guard, Veterans of the First World War, the British Legion, scouts, guides, the Salvation Army Band, and any one else who wanted to participate, marched in a mile-long Victory Parade from Carlisle Parade to Alexandra Park. The salute was taken at the War Memorial by the Mayor and a senior army officer. In all, 10,000 people gathered to watch and to join in a service of thanksgiving on the main lawn. In his speech there, the Mayor said, *'We have passed through the shadows and are now getting back into the sunlight'*.

On that bright May afternoon, the Mayor's words expressed what everyone felt. From the genteel tranquillity of pre-war years the people of Hastings had travelled together through the horrors of war. They had shared hardships, grief, separation, and restrictions of all kinds in their daily lives. Many of them had been seriouly injured. Others had lost loved ones and homes. There had been bravery, as well as less worthy behaviour, among those travelling companions. The children, in the wartime period, had been wrenched from their families, deprived of much of their schooling and had known little of the carefree days of normal childhood. On that day in Alexandra Park, as the journey ended, it was easy to appreciate the meaning of the Mayor's closing words, *'Incipit vita nova'* (Here begins a new life).

APPENDIX I

Main Private Schools in Hastings and St Leonards-on-Sea before the Second World War.

Buchanan College, Dane Road (closed).

Clyde House School, Sedlescombe Road North (now a Nursing Home).

Dunmore School, London Road (closed).

Exmouth House School, Exmouth Place (closed).

Glen View School, Clive Avenue (closed).

Gray's Preparatory School, Southwater Road (closed).

Hastings and St Leonards Ladies' College, Cumberland Gardens (closed).

Hollington Park School, Gillsman's Hill (closed).

Hurst Court Preparatory School, The Ridge (now a Conference Centre).

King's College, Hollington Park Road (closed).

Laton House School, Laton Road (closed).

Sacred Heart Convent, Old London Road (now a R.C. Primary School).

St Augustine's Convent, Filsham Road (school closed).

St Margaret's Ladies' School, The Ridge (now a Nursing Home).

Summerfields Preparatory School, Bohemia Road (premises and land acquired by Council. Law Courts, Police Station, Fire Station, Ambulance Station and other public buildings now occupy the site).

The Uplands School, Quarry Hill (now part of Hastings College of Arts & Technology).

Wellington College, Wellington Square (closed).

Westerleigh School, Hollington Park Road (still open).

Winton House School, Dane Road (closed).

APPENDIX II

Date items went on ration	
29 September 1939	National Register set up. Identity cards issued.
8 January 1940	Food rationing begins. Bacon, ham, sugar and butter.
March 1940	Meat rationed.
July 1940	Tea, margarine, cooking fats and cheese rationed.
March 1941	Jam, marmalade, treacle and syrup rationed.
June 1941	Distribution of eggs controlled.
August 1941	Extra cheese ration for manual workers introduced.
November 1941	Distribution of milk controlled.
December 1941	Points scheme for food introduced. National dried milk introduced.
January 1942	Rice and dried fruit added to points system.
February 1942	Canned tomatoes and peas.
April 1942	Breakfast cereals and condensed milk added to points system.
June 1942	American dried egg powder on sale.
July 1942	Sweets rationed.
August 1942	Biscuits added to points system.
December 1942	Oat flakes added to points system.
December 1944	Extra tea allowance for 70 year olds and over introduced.
January 1945	Whalemeat and snoek available for sale.
July 1946	Bread rationed.

The above information is published by kind permission of
J Sainsbury's archive department.

APPENDIX III

During World War II, most food-stuffs were rationed or on controlled distribution, and only small quantities were allocated. Recipes were devised which produced a pleasing result without using the most scarce ingredients. Here are two examples of wartime recipes.

BUN LOAF (very good)

Ingredients: 8 tablespoons SR flour
2 tablespoons golden syrup
1 tablespoon marmalade
2 small teaspoons gravy browning
2 tablespoons sultanas or dried peel or 1 of each
Half and half milk and water to mix

Method: Sift the flour into a bowl and stir in the fruit or peel, make a well in the centre, put in the syrup, browning and marmalade. Mix to a soft consistency with the milk and water. Turn into a 1lb loaf tin and bake at regulo $3\frac{1}{4}$ for $1\frac{1}{4}$ hours. Cut when perfectly cold. (This loaf will keep for up to a week in a tin.)

WOOLTON PIE (generally disliked)

Named after Lord Woolton the Minister of Food, this recipe is perhaps the only thing for which he is really remembered. The dish was useful in that it required no meat and, in the absence of anything better, was a great filler of empty stomachs.

Ingredients: 1lb each of 4 different vegetables such as potatoes, cauliflower, carrots, and swede. (Parsnips could be used if using mashed potatoes for the crust.)
1 teaspoonful Marmite (During the war Betox was used)
1oz porridge oats
1oz grated cheese
3 spring onions
salt and pepper

Method: Dice and boil the vegetables in a large saucepan until tender: strain, and keep about $\frac{3}{4}$ pint of the vegetable water. Arrange the vegetables in a very large pie dish or oven dish. Add the Marmite to the water with the oats. Cook until thickened and add seasoning. Pour some over the vegetables and add chopped spring onions. Top with potato pastry* or mashed potatoes. Sprinkle with the grated cheese.
Bake in a moderately hot oven until golden brown and serve hot with the rest of the gravy.

* Potato pastry is made with 8 tablespoons flour, 4 tablespoons mashed potato and 2oz fat. (This could be dripping). Blend potato and flour together. Soften the fat and blend in. Water is not usually needed for mixing. Form into a ball with floured hands and pat out on a floured board to the required size. Place over the vegetables.

APPENDIX IV

Operation Sealion.

Operation Sealion was the name given to the German plan to invade Great Britain following the fall of France in June 1940. It was planned for September or October using the 16th Army under Busch, and the 9th Army under Strauff. The 6 divisions of the 16th Army were to set out from an area stretching from Ostend to the Somme and would invade the SE coast between Ramsgate and Hastings, concentrating on Ramsgate, Folkestone and Bexhill. The 4 divisions of the 9th Army were to land between Brighton and Littlehampton. The plan aimed to encircle and besiege London before heading for the Midlands. Possible dates for the invasion were to have been either the 21st September of the 1st October. The reason why this plan was never put into action has never been fully explained. One theory is that Hitler wished to have Britain as an ally in his planned invasion of Russia. Another is that Goering's Luftwaffe failed to annihilate the RAF during the Battle of Britain, which was a pre-requisite to a successful invasion.

APPENDIX V

NEW OFFICIAL LIST of COUPONS NEEDED for CLOTHING and FOOTWEAR 1st JULY 1941

Here is your new reference list. Cut it out. It is the *official* record of the correct number of coupons for each rationed article, and it takes the place of earlier lists.

Garments not listed take the coupon rating of nearest like garment	Man	Woman	Child
Single texture mackintosh, raincoat overcoat, cape, cloak—unlined or saddle lined—other than woollen, leather or fur	9	9	7
Mackintosh, cape, raincoat—other than those above	16	15	11
Overcoat lining (detached)	7	7	4
Jacket, blazer, bolero blouse-type jacket—if lined and woollen, leather or fur	13	12	8
Jacket (including blouse, type), blazer—if unlined and not woollen, leather or fur	6	6	4
Jacket (including blouse type), blazer—other than those in the two categories above	10	10	6
Cardigan, sweater, jersey, jumper, pullover, waistcoat—with long sleeves, and woollen, leather or fur	8	8	5
Waistcoat, jumper, jersey, sweater, cardigan—other than those in previous item	5	5	3
Shirt†—if woollen	7		6
Shirt†—other than woollen; boys' woollen blouse	5		4
Blouse, shirt-blouse, shawl—if woollen		6	4
Blouse, shirt-blouse, shawl—other than woollen		4	3
Trousers, slacks, over-trousers, breeches—if woollen	8	8	6
Trousers, slacks, over-trousers, breeches—other than woollen	5	5	4
Shorts—if woollen	5	5	3
Shorts—other than woollen	3	3	2
Skirt, divided skirt—if woollen		6	4
Skirt, divided skirt—other than woollen		4	3
One-piece shelter suit,—if woollen	11	11	8
Men and boys' overall—other than woollen	6		4
Dressing- or bathing-gown—if woollen	8	8	6
Dressing- or bathing-gown—other than wool	6	6	5
Pyjama Suit, nightshirt	8	8	6
Nightdress		6	5
Combinations—if woollen	7		6
Combinations—other than woollen	5		3
Woollen vest; non-woollen vest with sleeves; woollen pants or trunks; non-woollen pants (long legs); cotton football jersey; bathing costume	4		2
Undergarment not elsewhere listed; athlete's vest	3		2
Pair of stockings, socks, bathing trunks—if woollen	3		1
Pair of socks—other than woollen; cotton swimming drawers	1		1
Collar, shirt-front†, pair of cuffs or sleeves, tie	1	1	1
4 handkerchiefs (each of area less than 1 sq. ft.)	1	1	1
2 *other* handkerchiefs (less than 2 ft. in length or breadth)	1	1	1
Scarf, pair of gloves or mittens	2	2	2
Pair of slippers, goloshes, rubber overshoes, plimsolls, football boots, and certain specialist sport shoes	4	4	2
Pair of rubber boots or overboots, sandals, rubber-soled canvas tennis shoes	5		2
Pair of boots, shoes, overboots—other than those in previous two categories	7		2
Pair of leggings, gaiters or spats	3	3	2
Dress, gown, frock—if woollen		11	8
Dress, gown, frock—other than woollen		7	5
Gym tunic, girl's skirt or bodice		8	6

*Sizes exempt from Purchase Tax.
†With or without collars attached

ISSUED BY THE BOARD OF TRADE

APPENDIX VI

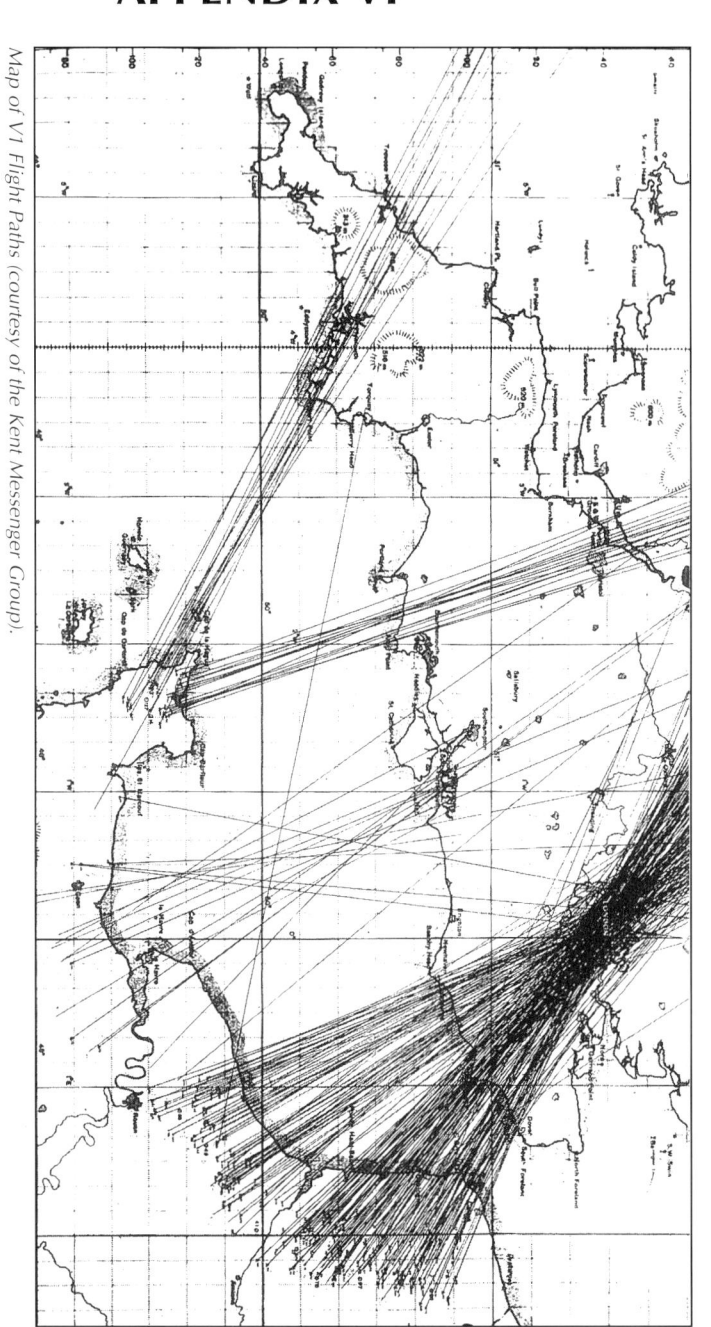

Map of V1 Flight Paths (courtesy of the Kent Messenger Group).

The above map has been reproduced by kind permission of Froglets Publications, Westerham, Kent

ACKNOWLEDGEMENTS

I wish to offer my thanks to the staff of Hastings Museum, Hastings Reference Library, Hastings Borough Council Tourism and Marketing Departments, Marriott's Photo Stores, and to the Editors of Hastings and St Leonards Observer and the Kent Messenger. Their help has always been willingly given and has been of immense value.

To all those who have generously lent photographs, searched their memories and given all kinds of assistance in the writing of this book I am most grateful. They are:

Dr F Ashworth, Mr S Benz, Mr Kevin Boorman, Mr Ken Brooks, Mr Dennis Collins, Mrs Diane Crouch, Miss Brenda Glazier, Lieutenant-Commander John Kennett, Mr Tom Lee, Mr Bob Ogley of Froglets Publications, Mr Chris Parkes, Mr M Rodgers, Mr Lyndon Rowe, Mr Brendan Salsbury, Mr Keith Scott, Mr D Spillett, Mr R J Stace, Miss Mabel Stringfellow, Mr Bob Tester, and Mr A W Wisden.

Every effort has been made, where possible, to trace copyright holders and to secure permission to reproduce illustrations.

Crown copyright material is reproduced with permission of the Controller of Her Majesty's Stationery Office.

BIBLIOGRAPHY

The Go-Between, by P L Hartley

Sussex Police Forces, Middleton Press

The History of Hastings Grammar School, by Baines, Conisbee & Bygate

Hastings Trolley Buses, Middleton Press

Hail and Farewell, Maidstone & District Motor Services Ltd.

Put That Light Out, by Mike Brown

How We Lived Then, by Norman Longmate

The Doodlebugs, by Norman Longmate

Doodlebugs and Rockets, Froglets Publications

Hastings & St Leonards in the Front Line, Hastings and St. Leonards Observer

Kelly's Directories

British Paddle Steamers, by Geoffrey Body

Fishermen of Hastings, by Steve Peak

Front Line 1940-1941, issued by the Ministry of Information

7th Canadian Reconnaissance Regiment in WW2, by Capt. Walter G Pavey

BBC Sound Archive Recordings

THE AUTHOR

Born in Hastings, Mary Haskell Porter grew up there during the 1930s and 1940s. She was educated in Hastings and Hertfordshire and later attended a private school in St Leonards-on-Sea. After a career in the Civil Service, she studied French as an external student at London University, and then took a diploma at the University of Lille before becoming a Member of the Institute of Linguists. Her later career was as a Lecturer in French Language and Bi-lingual Secretarial Studies. She is the author of two previous books on Hastings personalities, and enjoys writing light-hearted poetry.